An Armenian from Jerusalem

by Jacob (Hagop Khatcherian) Orfali

Ronin Publishing, Inc.
Berkeley, California

Published by:
Ronin Publishing, Inc.
Post Office Box 1035
Berkeley, California 94701

An Armenian from Jerusalem
ISBN: 0-914171-09-7

First printing 1987
Printed in the United States of America

Project editor: Sebastian Orfali
Copy editor, keyboarding: Judy Abrahms
Cover Design: Sebastian Orfali
Proofing , text layout and typography : Ginger Ashworth
Halftones, Cover art and layout: Norman Mayell

Dedication and Acknowledgement

This book is dedicated to the memory of my father and mother who spared no effort in giving us the best education possible. Their devotion and love made better persons out of their children.

Credit is due to our son Joseph Sebastian. He acted as a midwife for the realization of this work. He kept encouraging me and devoted many hours of his time, taking care of the typing and editing.

The idea of the book was conceived by our daughter Gabrielle. She wanted to know more about her dad and his Armenian ancestry.

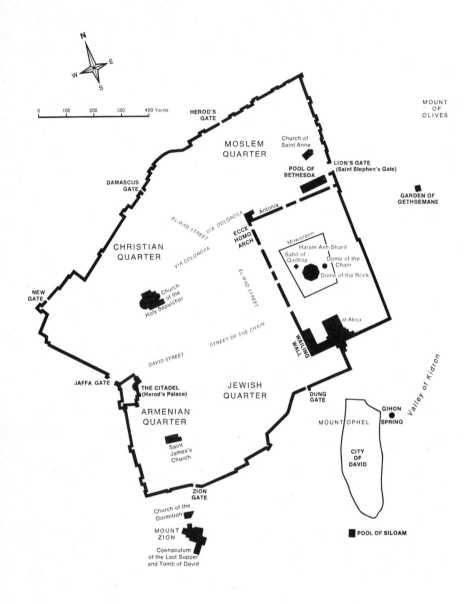

Map of the Old City of Jerusalem

Table of Contents

Outside the city walls of Jerusalem as it looked when Kevork first saw it during Ottoman Times, a Turkish flag flying over the city walls.

The Orfali Clan

Urfa is an ancient city in Eastern Turkey. According to tradition, Abraham lived in this city before moving to the promised land. Nearby is a river full of big healthy-looking carp. They can be seen moving in the crystal-clear water, unconcerned by the people swimming all around them. Nobody would dare touch them; they are considered sacred. According to legend, when Abraham saw these fish, he marveled at their gracious movements in the water, and he adopted them.

Urfa is famous for its contributions during the early stages of Christianity, when it housed many centers of learning, seminaries, and churches. Urfa was the home of the Syriacs, who still use the Aramaic language in their religious ceremonies, and the Armenians, the first nation to adopt Christianity. The Armenians became the Christian majority after the Syriacs failed due to internal quarrels and heresies. As a result, many of the Syriac parishes joined the Armenian church.

When the crusaders invaded the Middle East, they created three principalities in addition to the kingdom of Jerusalem. These were Antioch in Syria, Edessa (modern Urfa) in Armenia, and Tripoli in Lebanon. The Armenians thrived in these three kingdoms and were accorded many privileges not enjoyed by other minorities. Many noblemen among the crusaders married Armenian ladies; the first two queens of the Christian crusaders' kingdom of Jerusalem were Armenian princesses. The last Armenian king of Cilicia was related to the French kings by marriage. He is buried next to the French royalty in St. Denis, a suburb of Paris.

Baldwin of Boulogne was the third son of the Count of Boulogne. His paternal inheritance went to his eldest brother, Eustace. As a nephew, through his mother, of the Duke of Lower Lorraine, his second brother Godfrey inherited the duchy of his uncle. Baldwin, as the youngest son, was deprived of land. The motto of the feudal system was, "No land without a lord, no lord without a land." Without land, Baldwin had no hope of ever becoming rich and powerful. He joined the First Crusade in the hope of acquiring land and power in the East. Before the walls of Nicaea he befriended an Armenian noble named Bagrat (Pakrad). Bagrad was the brother of Kogh Vasil (Basil the Thief), the daring Armenian who had taken the fortresses of Kaisun and Rahan from the Turks. Instead of going to Jerusalem with his brother Godfrey of Bouillon and the other nobles, Baldwin followed Bagrad to Edessa, an ancient and powerful city, and became an ally of the Armenian ruling prince Thoros, son of Hethoum. Thoros had no children. He adopted Baldwin and designated him as his heir. When Thoros was killed by his vassals, Baldwin became by right and in fact lord of Edessa.

Baldwin married Arda (Archaluz), the daughter of Taphnuz (Thatul), the wealthiest Armenian lord. He surrounded himself with crusading lords and Frankish knights, preferring them to the local people. The Armenians had a higher level of civilization and religious tolerance. They were well aware of the country's politics. They bore in patience the outrageous behavior of their upstart ruler. In a few months, from a landless younger son, Baldwin had become a great lord, the overlord of a considerable domain. Within one year, at the head of Frankish and Armenian troops, he progressively eliminated the Turks from the land he made his own.

In the meantime the other knights marched on to Jerusalem. After a month's siege and terrible slaughter, Godfrey de Bouillon captured the city. Godfrey was elected "Defender of the Holy Sepulchre." He died in July 1100. His brother Baldwin came home from Edessa, and was crowned King of Jerusalem on Christmas Day, 1100. Baldwin le Bourg was Godfrey's cousin. He succeeded Baldwin de Bouillon as Count of Edessa. He married the Armenian princess Morphia, daughter of Gabriel Melitene. He later succeeded Baldwin I on the throne of Jerusalem as Baldwin II. Joscelin Courtenay, a brilliant knight, cousin of Baldwin le Bourg, was given the fertile land of Turbessel. He inherited the county of Edessa after the death of Baldwin I and the rise of Baldwin le Bourg to the throne of Jerusalem.

Joscelin married an Armenian princess, sister of Thoros I (lord of Vakha and grandson of Roupen I, founder of the Armenian dynasty in Cilicia). He took this tie seriously. Joscelin knew enough Armenian to communicate with his subjects, and he made himself loved by them. He treated his Armenian vassals as equal, as he would have treated his Frankish knights. Armenian historians have neither cruelty nor extortion to reproach him with.

In 1895 the Armenian Christians numbered one-third of the total population in Urfa, which had become part of the Turkish Ottoman Empire. In December of that year the Armenians suffered the cruelest and most devastating blow in their history. After a two-month siege of their quarter, the Armenian leaders obtained a truce from the army, which promised the return of normal life. Instead, the Turkish officer in charge ordered his troops to surround the cathedral, where the leaders and a large number of Armenians had taken refuge. Another contingent of soldiers, with a mob in their wake, rushed through the Armenian quarter. They plundered the houses and slaughtered all adult males after raping their wives and daughters in front of them. This occurred on a Friday. On the following Sunday the Turks attacked the cathedral, rifled its shrines, and set fire to the building. A crowd of women and children crouched inside, wailing with terror. All of them perished.

My father Kevork, or George, and his older brother Artin and younger sister Mariam, were among the survivors who had witnessed the atrocities. Hagop, my father's grandfather, saved young Kevork's life. When the Turkish mob broke into the house he feigned drunkenness and lay on top of the child sleeping in bed. The mob repeatedly stabbed the old man, killing him. Kevork, hiding under the body, could feel the blood dripping down onto him. After what he had experienced, my father swore not to remain under Turkish rule. His sister, who had seen the brutal mistreatment of her mother Yekhisapeth (Elizabeth) by the Turkish men, vowed never to marry, but to join a religious order.

When things quieted down, Yekhisapeth took charge of her husband's watermill. She was an energetic woman, spurred by her duty and devotion to her family. She not only succeeded in rebuilding the business, but made it a success. While her son Artin remained with her in the business, Kevork found himself a job as a cook's helper in an establishment that organized and supervised caravans.

Caravans were like the famous wagon trains of America. The caravan, with its many coaches, traveled under the leadership of a guide and an armed escort provided by the owner. Private coaches could join it by paying a fee for protection. These caravans stopped at inns, called "caravan sarai," for rest and for overnight stays (*sarai* means castle).

A caravan sarai had only one gate, large and very thick, with a small door cut in it, and a spy window through which any latecomers could be seen. The gate was closed at sunset, to be opened only at sunrise of the next day. The small door was sometimes opened for people to get through in emergencies. The gatekeeper lived in a small room next to the gate. Upon entering the inn, one saw a large yard surrounded by many doors that gave access to the travelers' living quarters, a kitchen, and a dining room. A separate area was reserved for the horses and carriages and the dwellings of the staff.

Kevork liked his job very much and learned a lot from the travelers, who were mostly foreigners: Englishmen, French, Germans, Americans, missionaries, scholars doing research, and businessmen. They were very friendly, and reciprocated his interest. It was a kind of schooling for him, preparing him for his future life.

After a few years of wandering, Kevork was hit in the face by a nervous horse while he was off guard, standing behind it. He was wounded above the left eye, which scarred him permanently. In later years, his left eye would sometimes refuse to focus properly.

While recuperating from this accident he had time to think. He resolved once again to leave Urfa, as he had vowed to do after the massacre. His younger sister Mariam was now in Jerusalem. She had applied for admission to the order of the Franciscan sisterhood, and had been referred to the French sisterhood of St. Joseph. This religious community had sent her to France, where she was ordained and sent to their convent in Bethlehem. When Kevork's mother heard of his decision, she told him that she too wanted to leave Urfa, to try to forget her awful experiences and to be near her daughter. She liquidated her business. Kevork, his mother, and his brother, accompanied by his brother's wife Sona and three children (Marie-Louise, Elizabeth, and Khatcher — "Christopher"), left Urfa for Jerusalem.

After visiting his sister, who was now known as Soeur Justine, a nun in the order of St. Joseph's convent of Bethlehem, they settled in Jerusalem, where for many centuries there had been a large Armenian community.

The Armenian Patriarch ("Archbishop") of Jerusalem is one of the three custodians of the Holy Land. The other two are the Latin Patriarch and the Greek Orthodox Patriarch. Brother Artin opened a business in Jerusalem, and Kevork became the private cook of the Latin Patriarch.

In addition to his seat in Jerusalem, the Latin Patriarch maintained a summer house in Beit Jala, a small seminary town near Bethlehem. In summer, when the Patriarch was in Beit Jala, Kevork went to the market each day to buy fresh food for the meals. Back at the summer house, he listened to the sermons of the seminarians as they practiced their skill on the cooks and kitchen help.

Many of Beit Jala's young men emigrated to Latin American countries because there was not enough work for them at home. Kevork met some of these young men as they prepared to leave for Colombia in South America. He joined them to realize a long-cherished dream.

In Colombia he changed his name to "Jorge de la Cruz," a translation of his Armenian name, Kevork Khatcherian. He accompanied some traveling salesmen — old-timers from Beit Jala who bought their wares in Bogotá, the capital city, and sold it in the rural areas — to learn the trade and the Spanish language.

Jorge easily picked up business Spanish; the Italian and Latin he had learned from the Patriarch and the seminarians helped him greatly. Being an Armenian, he was a born businessman and polyglot. Soon he was working on his own. While the other salesmen sold only for cash, he extended credit. He acquired many customers who liked his good manners, courteous behavior and constant smile. He always had a good word to say about his customers' children and their well-kept homes and gardens. They reciprocated by inviting him to join them in their meals and, since they knew he was a bachelor, offered to wash and mend his clothes. When they had no money to pay their debts on the appointed date, he accepted as payment precious and semi-precious stones that they had found in their fields. In this way, he unknowingly stumbled into a fortune.

The jewel merchant in Bogotá paid good money for the stones, and urged him to get more. Soon Jorge was bartering for anything his rural customers desired from the capital, bringing them these goods in exchange for their gems. He was so successful that he opened a large business specializing in ladies' laces that he imported directly from France, becoming sole importer and distributor for the French manufacturers. Needless to say, he continued to send money through his sister to help his mother in Jerusalem.

Now that he had a good income, he began thinking of starting a family of his own. He wanted some heirs to inherit what he had begun and perhaps to improve on it. He wrote to his mother about his intention and asked her to join him in Colombia, to help him find a bride and settle with the couple. She replied that he should come to Jerusalem. They would return to Urfa to get him a bride from one of the families they knew. Then they would all go back to Colombia. He wrote her again on this subject, but received no reply. After a long wait, he decided to travel to Jerusalem to investigate the cause of her silence.

When he arrived, Kevork could find neither his mother nor his brother and family. When he went to see his sister in Bethlehem, she informed him that his brother had died. His mother, with his brother's wife and children, had gone back to Urfa with the help of the Franciscan order, who are the Catholic custodians of the Holy Land and are in charge of the parish to which the family belonged. The religious leaders in the Middle East really do take care of their parishioners, helping them morally and financially when necessary.

Kevork took the next caravan to Urfa. After a happy reunion, his mother spread the word that her son Kevork, who had a good business in Colombia, was back in his native town looking for a bride to take with him to Colombia. According to the custom of the time, an eligible girl would be called to the house of a near relative early in the morning. There the groom's mother would see how she looked, get close to her, listen to her speech and find out whether she had body odor or mouth odor. Normally, once the girl had passed this examination, there would be a long-term engagement to let the couple become acquainted before getting married. In his case, Kevork wanted to get back to his business as soon as possible. A quick marriage was imperative.

Early one morning a girl named Hanum ("Lady" in English) was called urgently to her aunt's house. There Kevork's mother saw her for the first time, and took an immediate liking to her. There was only one problem: she had a smallpox scar on her left cheek. At the time, everybody in that part of the world had a smallpox scar somewhere, but Kevork had stated strongly that he did not want a girl with a pock mark on her face.

When Yekhisapeth came home, she told Kevork that she found the right bride for him, a girl from one of the prominent families of the Armenian community, very well-mannered, good-looking, and young. When Kevork saw her it was love at first sight. He said to his mother, "This is the girl for me!" His mother asked whether he had a good look at her face.

"Did you notice the pock mark on her left cheek?"

He replied, "It is not important. The other perfect features of her face, her beautiful eyes and lovely smile, won't allow the onlooker's eyes to wander to her cheek. I love her."

Yekhisapeth, accompanied by Hanum's aunt Hosana, went to see the girl's mother to ask her daughter's hand in marriage to her son. As is customary, Rhipsime, Hanum's mother, said,

"I have to talk the matter over with the other members of the family. Then I will send our answer."

That night the whole Arzuhaljian family met to discuss the future of their youngest daughter. First they told her that the young man she had seen at her aunt's house liked her and wanted to marry her. They asked for her reaction.

Hanum blushed and stammered. "I don't know," she said. "I will do what you say."

They knew she would have refused right away had she not had some good feelings for the young man, so they went on: "Would you object to becoming his wife? If you marry him, you will have to leave us all and go with him in a ship to a very far country called Colombia."

Hanum replied, "Is that not what the Holy Book says? A wife must leave her father, mother and family, follow her husband, and start her own family." The first hurdle had been passed.

Next came the question of religion. Kevork belonged to the Armenian Catholic church, affiliated with the Pope in Rome. The Arzuhaljians belonged to the Armenian Gregorian church, and were followers of the Catholicos (the Armenian Pope) in Etchmiazine in Armenia. But it would not be the first time a Gregorian Armenian had married an Armenian Catholic. The marriage of the Armenian princesses to the crusader noblemen was recalled, and this obstacle too was overcome.

It was very difficult for Hanum's mother to accept the separation from her youngest daughter, especially Hanum's departure for an unknown country so far away. At this point the family turned to the aunt in whose house it had all started. This lady was a soothsayer, and had predicted many things that eventually came to pass. She asked for a few minutes of silence, wetted her right thumb with saliva, and began to speak. "I see a very bright future for Hanum," she said, "in a far and beautiful country which is dear to many nations. She will be one of the few survivors of a very dark cloud that will end most of our lives. She will be happy and bear many children. Let her enjoy her destiny."

The next day, word was sent to the Khatcherian family that Hanum seemed destined to be betrothed to Kevork. Within a week, Kevork and Hanum were united in holy matrimony in a combined engagement and wedding ceremony, as is customary in such cases, thus dispensing with a long engagement.

Soon after, the happy young couple started preparing for their long journey with Yekhisapeth. They were suddenly faced with an unpleasant situation. Their sister-in-law Sona was supposed to stay in Urfa with her children in a new house they were buying for her. She changed her mind, saying, "You are my people. My children are your children. I am coming with you." Kevork felt compelled to take them along.

After getting on the road, their first real chance to recover from the weariness of travel came in Aleppo, Syria. They planned to spend a week there in a decent hotel before joining the next caravan to Jerusalem. They would visit the holy shrines in Jerusalem with the young bride and introduce her to Soeur Justine in Bethlehem.

While shopping in the Aleppo market with Yekhisapeth, Hanum had a glimpse of her oldest brother, John, seated in a carriage that sped by. She started shouting, "That's my brother John! Mother, please stop the carriage!"

Yekhisapeth tried to calm her, telling her to stop behaving like a child. "You must be mistaken; it could not be your brother."

Hanum refused to calm down. Back at the hotel, she rushed to Kevork in agitation. She insisted she had seen her brother John in the carriage. She asked Kevork to go and look for him. Kevork promised that if it was really John she had seen, he would not come back without him. He left the hotel and went straight to the coffeehouse where all the out-of-town Armenians congregated. Sure enough, he saw John, surrounded by other Armenian young men, apparently discussing a serious matter. John rushed over to Kevork as soon as he saw him, and they embraced. Kevork said, "What a pleasant surprise, brother! Hanum saw you in the carriage and sent me to look for you. What brings you to Aleppo?"

John replied, "I cannot talk about it in public. I will tell you everything when we get to your hotel." After John promised to meet his friends later, they were on their way.

In the meantime Hanum was busy. She prepared food and set a table worthy of a king. This traditional Armenian table included all kinds of snacks such as shish-kebab, hummus (a paste made from chick peas), fried chicken, baba ghanush (an eggplant mixture), pistachios, sardines, small Armenian pizzas, different salads, boiled eggs, caviar, green and black olives, Romaine lettuce, peanuts, salted pumpkin seeds, ground parsley mixed with sesame butter, pita bread cut in quarters, and so on. In the center of the table stood a large vase full of flowers, a couple of bottles of Arack (anise brandy), and a bucket of ice. When Kevork and John arrived at the hotel, Hanum rushed to embrace John with tears of joy in her eyes, saying, "I knew it was you, John!" She could not stop kissing — "these kisses are for the other members of the family."

After the ritual toasting, while sipping Arack and nibbling at the snacks, John began his tale. He said, "I am secretary-treasurer of the Armenian Defense League, which is known as a cultural and sports organization for young Armenians. Our real aim is to prevent the recurrence of what happened in December of 1895 when we were cheated by the Turkish Army, who promised us peace, and instead slaughtered us like sitting ducks and raped our women. How can we ever forget the sheiks who threw a group of Armenian youths down on their backs facing Mecca and cut their throats, one by one, while reciting verses of the Koran as if they were sacrificing sheep? Or the other group of Armenians who, when they refused to become Moslems, were hanged and told with derision, 'Let your Christ save you to prove that he is a greater prophet than Mohammed!'

"We are training our young men in small groups in the villages, which we still have from the time when our ancestors were feudal lords. They are now run by some Kurdish tribes who supply us with milk, cheese, butter, fruits and vegetables and Easter lambs. They keep the rest for themselves."

Hanum interrupted him: "Those are lovely places! We used to spend the hot summer vacation months there. I have fond memories of the green fields, the fruit trees, the lambs jumping in the meadows. The whole family having a good time playing games and some enjoying hikes, eating fruits directly from the trees, and catching large delicious fish swimming in the lazy river — it really felt like paradise."

John took up his story again. "You know our name is Arzuhaljian [court petitioners]. One member of our family still holds that position in court. Many people envy us this post and our villages. Last week the district commissioner, a good friend of the family, came to our house in the dark of the night and spoke to me secretly. He said that I must have some enemies who had written to the capital, Istanbul, accusing me of being the leader of an organization that plots to overthrow the government. He had received orders for my immediate arrest to stand trial for that accusation. He advised me to skip town right away, since the order of arrest applies only to Urfa for the present. Actually, if I can leave the country I will be safe. That is why I am in Aleppo, on my way to the U.S.A. to join some Armenian sponsors of our organization."

Kevork said, "I am sad at the news of your problems, but we are happy to see you again before you leave. I am sure you will do very well in America. We wish you the best of luck. We promise to say a special prayer for you at the tomb of the Savior on our pilgrimage to Jerusalem. But let's not forget practical matters. Do you need any help financially or otherwise? Don't hesitate to ask — what we have is yours."

"As a matter of fact," John said, "I was trying to get a loan when you saw me at the coffeehouse. My departure from Urfa was so sudden that the family didn't have enough time to raise money for my long trip."

Kevork gave him the sum he needed. John thanked him heartily for saving him from an awkward situation, and promised to pay him back as soon as possible.

After a short stay in Aleppo, they went their separate ways, John to take a ship bound for the U.S., and the others to their next stop in Jerusalem in the Holy Land.

Uncle John Arzuhaljian (mother's brother) became a successful business man in Chicago. Kevork and Hanum saw him for the last time in Aleppo, on their way to Jerusalem.

Armenian farmers dressed in Ottoman Turkish garb, on a visit to the "big" town of Urfa.

Artin Arzuhaljian (Hanum's brother) in his Turkish sergeant's uniform.

The courtyard of an ancient caravan sarai (inn).

Gate to the ancient caravan sarai.

The Move to Jerusalem

Jerusalem sits on a rocky plateau in the Judaean hills at an average altitude of 2,500 feet above the Mediterranean Sea. The mean annual temperature of Jerusalem is 62.8° F, with a maximum of 112°F and a minimum of 25° F. Its average annual rainfall is about 22.4 inches, and occurs mostly between November and April. From May to October is the dry season. In summer the heat is softened by a sea breeze and the temperature usually falls sharply at night. In spring and autumn an oppressive hot wind blows across Jerusalem. It is called "Khamsin," which means "fifty" in Arabic. It normally occurs for fifty days in every year and makes life exceedingly miserable, especially at night when people want to sleep and cannot.

The city was originally built by the Canaanite priest Melchizedek ("Righteous King"), who erected the first temple and officiated in it as a priest of God. He gave it the name of Jerusalem ("Yerushala'im," City of Peace). King David of the Jews expelled the Canaanites and colonized it with his own people. It has ever since been called the City of David.

Jerusalem has been called by many different names: the City of David, the City of Peace, the Holy City, the Regicide City (killer of kings), and most recently, by the Israelis, Jerusalem the Golden. Throughout history the old city was protected by a thick fortified wall. It was destroyed by the enemy and rebuilt by its defenders many times over the ages. The present wall was built by the Ottoman Sultan Selim I in 1517.

The city wall has many gates in the various parts of town. In ancient times these gates were closed at sunset and opened at sunrise the next day. People caught outside the gates after sunset ran the risk of being robbed and killed by night marauders. There were caravan sarais, or inns, inside the city. Two of them can still be visited by the modern traveler. One of the caravan sarais, the Inn of the Copts, is located on the way to the Holy Sepulchre. In the courtyard of this inn there is a pool where Bathsheba was swimming when King David first saw her from his nearby citadel. The other caravan sarai, the Inn of the Sultan, is located in the Street of Chain on the way to the Solomon's Temple place.

The various churches maintain their own compounds to house pilgrims on their travels to the Holy Land. The

Armenian Gregorians have the St. James' convent on Mount Zion, with living quarters for many thousands. This convent is now occupied by children of the survivors of the first genocide of the Twentieth Century, perpetrated in 1915 by the Turks against their Armenian subjects. There is also an Armenian quarter outside the convent, where the permanent Armenian inhabitants of Jerusalem have dwelt for many centuries.

The Greek Orthodox have many convents to house their faithful. The Copts, descendants of the early Egyptian Christians, have the large convent of St. Mark in the vicinity of the Holy Sepulchre. The Abyssinians maintain their own small place. The Russians have a compound outside the city wall, as well as a church near the Latin garden of Gethsemane. The Moslems maintain many rooms for their pilgrims in their temple compound. The Catholics have Notre Dame de France, a huge hostelry outside the New Gate, and the Casa Nova inside the city walls.

When Kevork's group reached Jerusalem, they stayed at the Armenian Catholic convent in the Via Dolorosa ("Way of the Cross") near the sites of the third and fourth Stations of the Cross. After their visits to the various holy shrines in the land and their numerous get-togethers with Soeur Justine, they decided not to leave, because by now Hanum was with child and they did not want to risk the long sea voyage.

At this time, Kevork adhered to an old proverb — "Money is like dirt on your hands which will wash off with water, whereas a profession will stay with you forever." He decided to learn an additional trade from the local Armenians. He learned how to make halvah, a sweet food composed mainly of sesame butter and syrup, commonly called Turkish Delight.

Then what Kevork most dreaded came to pass. He was called to military service as a native of the Ottoman empire. He was deferred in exchange for a sum of money, as was customary in those days, but was not allowed to leave the country. Kevork was obliged to open his own candy and halvah factory to sustain his family. A Turkish census clerk, who had trouble spelling Khatcherian, asked what city they came from. When they replied "Urfa," he entered the name Orfali on their papers.

After a while Kevork was called again to military service and once again he redeemed himself with a payment of money. But when he was called for the third time, he had to go, as money could redeem him no longer. He ended up as cook and interpreter to a high Turkish officer in the vicinity of Istanbul, the capital.

Grandmother Yeghisapeth, who had now two daughters-in-law and her grandchildren to look after, took charge of the candy factory. She ran it as smoothly as if she had done nothing else all her life. She acted not as a boss to the workers, but rather as a mother. She counseled them and helped them solve their problems. They rewarded her with loyalty, so her work became easy and was crowned with success.

Yeghisapeth spent New Year's Eve of 1915 with her daughter Soeur Justine in the St. Joseph convent in Bethlehem. She awaited the birth of her second grandchild to Hanum, who was due any day now. (Hanum had already borne a son, Joseph, on the feast of St. Joseph in April 1913.) I was born shortly after midnight of December 31, 1914. Though Yeghisapeth was back in Jerusalem early in the morning on January 1, 1915, she was too late to assist at my birth.

Meanwhile, there was a change in the government of the Ottoman Empire. The last sultan was replaced by a triumvirate of three young Turkish officers. At the head was Enver Pasha, assisted by Jemal Pasha and Talast Pasha, members of the Young Turks' Committee. Before coming to power, the members of this committee had been helped by Turkish Armenians while they lived in exile in European capitals such as Paris and Rome. There was jubilation when the "Young Turks" took over. The mufti (the Moslem religious leader), along with the religious leaders of other communities — the Chief Rabbi, the Armenian Patriarch, and others — took part in the procession through the festively decorated streets of Istanbul. These officers, however, soon turned into fanatic Turks. They forgot their promises of social reform, and of equal treatment for all those born in Turkey, regardless of religion and ethnic origin.

Enver Pasha, who was married to an Ottoman princess, had secret designs. He dreamed of filling the chair of the Sultan one day. He turned out to be a worse Armenian-hater than the bloody Sultan Abdul Hamid, who had ordered the slaughter of the Armenians in the 1880s.

At the start of the First World War, Enver vowed to solve the "Armenian question" for all time. He ordered the annihilation of one and one-half million Armenians. He falsely accused them of spying for and helping the Russian Christian enemy with whom Turkey was at war. In fact, the Armenians had no use for the Russians; the Russians did not care for the Armenians either, since the latter refused to join the Russian Orthodox Church whose head was the Czar of Russia (just as the British monarch is the head of the Anglican church).

At this time the Armenians were given the choice of converting to Islam or facing torture and death. They refused to accept Islam. They were proud of belonging to the first nation converted to the Christian faith by St. Gregory the Illuminator in the early Fourth Century.

The Turks could not understand the attitude of the Armenians. Their nomadic founding fathers, who came from the steppes of Turkestan, would readily have accepted the Christian faith. But the Church of Rome had imposed many conditions which the Turks considered too humiliating to their pride, so instead they had adopted Islam, which was easier to digest.

Orders were sent from Istanbul to arrest all Armenian males above a certain age, under the pretext of preventing them from staging an armed uprising. The Turks assembled all the women and children and herded them on foot, under armed guard, toward the Deir Ezzor desert in Syria. The official explanation was that they were being relocated so that they would not be able to help the enemy. They were also promised that the menfolk would follow. They were allowed to carry only a bare minimum of their belongings with them.

The Turks slaughtered the men before even the march began, and the mounted militia drove the women and children very hard. They were not allowed to rest during the day, nor to get enough sleep during the night. The women and children soon started to fall by the roadside, too exhausted to keep up, and most perished. The very small number who made it to the end were kept in the open, in a camp without protection from the burning sun, and with no water to drink. They envied their companions who had fallen dead on the way.

The Armenians serving in the military were disarmed and were ordered to dig trenches and to perform other hard labor. They were eventually liquidated at the discretion of their officers.

My grandmother had a nephew, her only sister's son, by the name of Hagop, or Jacob. He was serving in the Turkish army. She heard that while resting from the exhausting work of digging trenches in the midday heat, he fell asleep and his guard crushed his head with a large rock. When I was baptized a few days later, I was given his name.

This was a trying period in the life of our family in Jerusalem. We heard all kinds of rumors about the fate of the members of our family in Urfa, and about the other Armenians in Turkey. Though we were not harmed in Jerusalem, we did not know what the future might bring. We had not heard from my father for a long time and we did not dare to speculate about his fate.

To top all this off, a delegation of Turkish military and police officers went around to all the houses, confiscating the jewelry and copperware. In exchange, they presented award certificates praising the owners' patriotic contributions to the war effort. When they came to our house, my grandmother managed to rescue some cooking pots and one spoon for each of us. All our other pots, pans, dishes, and trays, our antique open fire charcoal heating stove, and so on, were hauled away. Luckily, the Turks were so blinded by the quantity of loot they got from us that they overlooked a back room, where we had stored the copper cauldrons that we used for making halvah and other candy.

General Allenby, better known as Lord Allenby, gained a victory over the Turks in Gaza in November 1917. This led to the capture of Jerusalem on December 9, 1917. Allenby rode to the Jaffa Gate of the old city. After dismounting from his horse, he walked through the Gate and was welcomed as a liberator by the city notables and the heads of the various religions.

His walk through the gate was a symbolic gesture that meant he came as a friend. In contrast, when Kaiser Wilhelm II had visited Jerusalem in the 1890s, the Turks had made a breach in the wall next to the Jaffa, and built a road so that the German Kaiser could enter the old city , riding a white horse.

After receiving reinforcements, General Allenby defeated the enemy at Megiddo in September 1918 and captured Damascus and Aleppo. Har Megiddo (from the Hebrew, meaning "mountain or hill of Megiddo") has been the scene of many historic battles. It is referred to as Armageddon in the Bible (Revelations XVI, 16), the place where the forces of God will do battle with the kings of the earth who are under the leadership of the devil (Revelations XIX, 11-21).

After the defeat of the Turks by Allenby we received news from my father through the Red Cross. He had been captured by the British forces in Gaza, where he had ended up with his officer, and was now a prisoner of war in Egypt. Shortly after the letter arrived, a British military officer, accompanied by an interpreter, came to see my mother. He told her that my father had petitioned for a release from the prisoner-of-war camp. As an Armenian he had a good chance for freedom. While in Egypt he had been active in recruiting volunteers for an "Armenian Liberation Legion." The Legion fought with the Allied Forces under General Allenby and played a vital role in the defeat of the Turks. The Armenians who had fallen while serving the Allied Forces are buried in a common grave in the Armenian Cemetery on Mt. Zion, Jerusalem. This is called the Monument of the Martyrs, in memory of all the Armenians who died at the hands of the Turks. Special prayers and patriotic speeches are made there each year.

The British officer's mission was to ask whether my mother was ready to take my father back. "What a question!" said my mother. "Kevork is my husband and the father of my children. Everything we possess was provided by him. Of course I want him back!"

The Jaffa Gate, showing the moat that was filled and the walls that were breached by the Turks to enable Kaiser Wilhelm II to enter the city without dismounting his horse.

George (Kevork) and Hanum proudly show their firstborn son, Joseph, accompanied by cousin Marie Louise.

Back row, from left: Father Kevork with newly arrived Uncle Artin, his sister Hosanah, cousin Christopher and his sister Marie Louise.

Front row, seated: Grandmother Yeghisabeth with mother Hanum and her three firstborn sons Joseph, Jacob and Levon.

Never a Dull Moment!

Shortly after the visit of the British liaison officers to our house, we rejoiced in welcoming Father back to Jerusalem. He immediately took over the business Grandma Yeghisapeth had preserved. The family peace was soon shattered by Father's widowed sister-in-law. After dating her son's teacher, a Lebanese Christian widower, she married him with the family's blessing. A few months later, she deserted her husband and children. She went to live with a newly arrived Armenian man. As a result Grandma Yeghisapeth told Father, "I know the house is not big enough to accommodate the three children of your deceased brother in addition to your growing family. Therefore I've decided to rent a house as a home for the three poor orphans."

She then left our house but she accepted no financial help from Father. She started her own business. She visited homes carrying samples of novelties and fine ladies' clothing, and took orders for later delivery. She did very well for herself, but the abandoned children felt out of place without their mother. At this time it was decided that the two girls, Marie-Louise and Elizabeth, should go to the orphanage section of the boarding school of the Sisters of St. Joseph in Bethlehem, where my aunt Justine was a nun. The boy, Khatcher, was accepted by the Franciscans in their orphanage, where the students were offered industrial training in their various workshops. Khatcher opted for mechanical training and excelled in it later in life. He also joined the chorus group "Escola Cantore," which sang in solemn masses and religious services, in shrines all over the Holy Land. In addition he joined the Franciscan Fathers' musical band, in which he played clarinet.

In the meantime, we heard from Haroutioun (nicknamed Artin), one of our mother's brothers. He was a very restless young man, full of mischief. The family was very relieved when he joined the regular Turkish army before World War I. Even though he was Armenian, being in the regular army saved his life. He wrote to us from Aleppo, and my father sent him money and the necessary travel papers, and he came to Jerusalem. Our family received him with joy. We had no near relatives in Jerusalem and he filled the gap. He was a likable person, with blue eyes and blond hair. Father was pleasantly impressed by Uncle Haroutioun and offered him a partnership in an import business in which Uncle would travel to Syria and Egypt to buy dried fruits, candied almonds, and Turkish delight directly from the producers and ship them to Jerusalem. The venture did not succeed financially. In Aleppo he met Rosa, an Armenian girl he knew from Urfa, and got engaged to her. Father again helped our prodigal uncle. He entrusted him with the family retail grocery shop, which was in David's Street, the best location for business. Father then rented a big place in the Christian quarter, where he started a halvah and candy factory. The factory also had enough room to store goods for the grocery shop. After a few months my uncle's fiancée was sent for and they got married in the Armenian Gregorian Church on Mount Zion. My parents were both happy to see Haroutioun finally settled down.

A short while later, he proposed to my father that the retail grocery shop be transferred to him at a mutually agreeable price, to be paid in monthly installments to my father. Mother was furious at her brother's nerve. Father decided to close the candy factory, and took over the grocery store. Uncle's best man at his wedding was in the business of used clothing imported from America. He helped Uncle to go into the same business and open a store. Before this happened, there were some racial riots in Jerusalem. A curfew was imposed and a crier went around (since there was no other effective means of communication), warning people to stay indoors and to stay away from open windows. On one of these occasions, my father was trying to block an opening in the wall with a flower pot. The opening was on top of the door to the house. Whenever there was knocking at the door, we looked out through this opening to see who was there. My father was detected by a sentry in the street. Upon seeing a suspicious movement at the opening, the sentry fired a warning shot in the air. The bullet ricocheted from the wall of a neighbor's house and struck my father in the head. We were lucky to have Uncle Haroutioun in the house, for he rushed into the street shouting for help. He accompanied my father in an ambulance to the Rothchild Hospital (later renamed "Hadassah") in the Prophets' Street. We experienced an agonizing time of uncertainty about my father's fate. Imagine our relief when Uncle returned with the news that the bullet had not damaged the brain. It was lodged between the skull and the skin of the head. Father was released from the hospital within a week.

Since Haroutioun did not have money to start a new business, Mother asked Father whether he had given any money for the business to get Uncle off his back. Father neither admitted nor denied this.

At about this time we heard from three sisters of my mother. They wrote that they were saved by the Kurdish people who took care of the family village. The Kurds protected them and provided for their needs. At the time of writing, they were acting as mothers to the surviving Armenian children at the orphanage of the American Foundation for Relief of the Near East. Once again Father opened his purse. He sent them money and the necessary travel documents, and welcomed them to Jerusalem.

We lived at the edge of the Armenian Quarter, in a rented house. All the resident Armenians, as well as members of all other resident communities, lived in their separate quarters in houses provided to them by the administrative offices of their respective communities. Families that had to live outside their communities' quarters due to lack of housing or for convenience got cash to cover their rent. The Armenians who flocked to Jerusalem, fleeing the Turkish genocide, were housed in the Armenian convent where the pilgrims used to stay. The premises were not designed for permanent residences, and the facilities were very primitive.

When my mother's sisters, Masrur with her two sons Archak and Armenaq, Khambag with her son Sarkis and daughter Rachel, and Hosanna (who was unmarried), came to Jerusalem, they were accommodated in the Armenian convent. Uncle Artin also lived there after he started his own business. We needed a bigger house, with storage space for the stock of the grocery after Father gave up the candy factory. We moved to the Street of Chains ("Hart el Sinsileh"), near the mosque of the Dome of the Rock in the temple place.

To earn a living my aunts Masrur and Khambag mended and cleaned used clothes imported from America before they were sold. Later they did fine Armenian needlework, which was sold in the American Colony antique stores in Jerusalem and the United States. Archak worked as an apprentice shoemaker, Armenaq and Sarkis were placed in the Salisian Fathers' technical school, "Don Bosco" in Bethlehem, Armenaq to learn custom shoemaking and Sarkis electrical engineering. Rachel went to the St. Joseph Sisters' orphanage in Bethlehem. Aunt Hosanna married an Armenian refugee from Urfa, who had his own shoe business.

My mother had always wanted a daughter. When my brother Levon was born, she let Levon's hair grow long, combed it for hours and braided it, until he was of school age. Dikran was born next. Then came Archark and finally we had my sisters, Elizabeth (Mignonette) and Nelly. With my oldest brother Joseph and myself, we were now five brothers and two sisters.

I have fond memories of life in Jerusalem as we children grew up. Our father was a very hard worker. He left early in the morning to be at the grocery in time for the delivery of bread from the bakery. He closed shop at 8 P.M. When we were old enough, we relieved him at noon so he could go home to have lunch and rest. Father bought us a parrot, named Coco, which was green with shades of yellow and red in its wings and on its head. Coco spoke and sang songs in Spanish. Father, who had learned Spanish in Colombia, had long conversations with him. Coco was a character. He playfully pinched the arms of unsuspecting ladies with his beak and laughed loudly at their screams, shouting "Surprise!" Whenever he saw a young beautiful girl, he addressed her with endearing words in a passionate tone.

Coco loved the rain. He opened his wings and danced on the clothesline, singing as he moved from one end to the other. Whenever we children cried, he joined us. When he was asked why he cried, he replied, "I am sad because my friend — " (here he would give the name of the child) " — is unhappy."

Coco was a terror for cats. People didn't buy cat food, so the cats sneaked into houses through the windows and took off with whatever they could find. But no cat came near our house. Coco attacked them with his sharp beak and whenever they ran away, he jeered and whistled after them.

We also had a dog named Job. Job was completely housebroken and slept in the kitchen. He never came near the table while we had our meals. He would eat whatever he was given. Sometimes it was only bread. It was an Armenian custom to buy a newly born lamb every December, raise it, fatten it, and have it ready for the Easter holidays. Our lambs were always called Prince in memory of the Prince of Peace, whose sufferings, death and resurrection are celebrated by Christians on Easter. Lambs are lovable creatures. We had lots of fun with ours. Mother would give them a hot bath whenever their soft, shiny white fleece got dirty. The lambs submitted readily to her scrubbing and seemed to enjoy it. We took our lamb with us to the fields around Jerusalem. He jumped, danced, and ran about with joy when we let him loose in the fields. Sometimes, when one of the children leaned over to pick flowers, the lamb could not resist giving us a butt in the rear. Our dog Job also followed us on these outings. Both creatures had fun chasing each other in their play.

We ate all our evening meals together. After the meal, Father spoke to us about his travels, his war experiences, and his life in Urfa as he was growing up. He told us stories with moral endings, such as the *Tales of the One Thousand and One Nights*. He never failed to tell us, or read to us, Bible stories once a week. We were thus introduced to Abraham's migration from Ur to the land of Canaan, to Loth, Sodom and Gomorrah, Ishmael, Isaac, Jacob and Esau. We learned of Joseph in Egypt, Moses and the Exodus, Samson, David and Solomon, and of course the New Testament as well.

We children pitched in whenever our help was needed. We shelled almonds for the grocery store. We ground various kinds of nuts in a small hand-operated stone mill. The ground nuts were mixed with powdered thyme to make an invigorating meal (Za'tar) eaten at breakfast. People first dropped a piece of bread in olive oil, rubbed it in Za'tar and ate it with coffee, milk or tea. We carried grocery goods from the warehouse to the store whenever Jabrin, our stockboy, was unavailable. My mother made all kinds of jams and preserves from apricots, quince, plums, and cherries. She also concentrated the juices of oranges, lemons, pomegranates, sour grapes (a substitute for lemon juice), and tomato sauce. She poured a layer of melted beeswax on top of each full jar and bottle to keep the preserves from spoiling. Since we had no refrigerator, my mother cut a whole sheep in pieces, cooked the pieces all together, and preserved the meat in deep fat from the melted fat of the sheep's tail. The meat thus preserved could be kept for a long time. Some beef was hung in a shady breezy spot to dry (like beef jerky). It was then covered with a paste of chili mix to make pasterma. Thinly sliced pasterma is better than any cold cuts sold in delicatessen stores. It was introduced to Poland by Armenians who immigrated to that country. In Poland it is eaten without its outer skin of chili paste. It is called "pastrami." Other kinds of meat were ground, mixed with spices and garlic, and put under heavy weights between wooden planks to make soujouk, or summer sausages.

Mayrigue was an old Armenian lady from Mouche. A survivor of the Holocaust, she had found her way to Jerusalem. She was hired to help our mother with her chores, but she became a member of the family. Her life experiences as a slave to a Kurdish family would fill an entire book. She wept bitterly whenever she remembered how, after the Turks forced them into a raging river, she pushed her own son underwater and drowned him rather than let him fall into the hands of slave traders. She herself was bloated when found unconscious on the riverbank by her future master.

When I came home one day, I heard heartbreaking sounds from the kitchen where my mother was cooking — sad singing interrupted by sobs. She was drowning her deep, painful sorrows in melodies and tears. Her sisters (my aunts) visited my mother that day. They must have discussed the fate of the members of their family who were slaughtered by the Turks. The Armenian community of Urfa (Edessa) was one of a few communities that decided to defend themselves rather than get slaughtered like docile sheep. My uncle Levon was one of the resistance organizers. His younger brother Garabed, an adolescent, carried ammunition hidden in baskets of fruits and vegetables to the Armenian fighters. When the Turkish army resorted to cannons against them, they were arrested while fleeing down the city wall on ropes. Levon was hanged with his comrades and Garabed — who was a very handsome boy with big blue eyes and shoulder-length blond hair — was kidnapped. This was the final blow to my maternal grandmother Rhipsime. She did not survive.

The Young Turks, in their struggle against the corrupt old Sultan's regime, were assisted by wealthy Armenians and Armenian organizations in the European capitals where they operated. They promised to grant some kind of semi-autonomy to the Armenians of Turkey after they took over the government.

The Young Turks overthrew the old Ottomans in 1908 and formed the ITTIHAD (Ittihad), a union government. Their motto could have been "E pluribus unum," since the Ottoman Empire comprised many different racial minorities. On this occasion there was a victory parade in the streets of Istanbul, the capital. The Armenian patriarch, the Jewish chief rabbi and the Moslem sheikh Ul Islam participated in it together in a horsedrawn carriage.

A triumvirate government was formed, headed by Enver Pasha, with Talaat Bey and Jamal Pasha assisting him. Under the Sultan, a figurehead, Enver was consort of imperial princess Nadjieh Sultana, the Sultan's daughter. He was an unimposing man, standing a diminutive five feet tall. His aspirations were great. In his office he displayed the portraits of Frederick the Great and Napoleon, both small men like him. Talaat was a minor official in the Post and Telegraph Office. Jamal was a career army officer. On a military campaign in the Caucasus, Enver panicked when surrounded by Russian soldiers. He was saved by Armenian soldiers of the Turkish army, who smuggled him out.

At the outbreak of World War I, rather than keep the party's promise, Enver decided to destroy the Armenians in Turkey instead of giving them semi-autonomy, and thus solve what he called the "Armenian question." He accused the Armenians of aiding the Russian enemy. Orders were sent from Istanbul to all the provinces for the arrest of all the Armenian men. They were never heard from again. The women and children were given twenty-four hours to get ready to march on foot, carrying a minimum of their belongings, to the Syrian deserts of Deir Ezzor. Most of them did not make it. They fell like flies on the roads, thirsty, hungry, and too exhausted to walk. The guards, who accompanied them on horseback, constantly prodded their unfortunate victims to keep moving on schedule. Those who fell were left behind to face the human vultures who followed the marchers and subjected the fallen to all kinds of atrocities. The tiny number who reached Deir Ezzor envied those who fell behind. They were tortured by the extreme heat of the desert and the lack of food and water. With no shelter from the scorching sun, they longed for death as if for a friendly rescuer.

Detailed sworn statements of the Armenian Holocaust, made by such consular personnel of the world powers as Henry Morgenthau, U.S. Ambassador to Turkey, were sent to their respective governments. These are kept in the official archives in Washington, Berlin, and other capitals.

At the end of World War I the victorious Allies recognized, in the peace treaty of Sevres on August 10, 1920, the Armenian republic created on the ashes of the historic Armenian provinces. However, the special interests of the Allies were stronger than justice. They created and armed a new Turkey under Mustapha Kemal Pasha. He attacked the infant Armenian republic at the end of September 1920, destroyed it, and subjected its people to another Holocaust.

The Turks were a semi-nomadic Central Asian people of Mongol origin. They came to Asia Minor as mercenaries of the Abbasid Persian Empire, imposed on its domain, took possession of Syria and Mesopotamia. The Turks were reputed to be as barbarous as they were invincible. Their advance in successive waves was similar to that of the Normans in Europe. They converted to Islam, though less out of faith than for convenience. The older Moslem nations were suspicious of their motives and feared them. When they began to encroach on the dominion of the Byzantine Empire, the Greek Emperor Alexius Comnenus requested the help of the Western Christians through Pope Urban II. This was an unwise step, as the Norman Christian leaders, in their so-called Crusades, turned the troubles of Byzantium to their profit by robbing the Empire of its possessions, and conspired with the Turks in their fight against the Byzantine Empire. In the end the Turks succeeded in expelling the Western Christians and conquered the weakened Byzantines. They created the Ottoman Empire. The Ottomans were like locusts. They overran countries that were green and fertile, such as Syria and Palestine, and turned them into semi-deserts.

We had no city water in our house. Some water was pumped to Jerusalem from Ein Arrub by way of "King Solomon's Pool" (on the way to Hebron), and from Ein Fara near Jerusalem. These two sources were not enough to fill the needs of the city. Much later the whole city got plenty of water, pumped from Ras El Ein near Tel Aviv. In ancient times, Herod the Great, King of the Jews, built a superb city with luscious gardens at this location and called it Antipatris in memory of his father.

Our main source of water was a cistern filled with rainwater. In the rainy season, gutters channeled the water from the roof into the cistern. The first rain was not allowed to reach the cistern, since it carried the dust and other dirt accumulated on the roof during the long dry summer. We drew the water from the cistern with buckets and stored it in large earthenware jars for our daily use.

Every Thursday it was the children's job to draw the water and put it into large storage barrels for use the next day. Friday was laundry and baking day. The water was heated in large copper cauldrons over a wood fire. We had to use water sparingly. When the rainfall was inadequate and our cistern ran out, we bought water from water carriers, who brought it in goatskins from an inexhaustible underground lake in the temple place, which must have been built at the time of Solomon.

Houses in the old city did not look attractive from the street. Yet our living quarters were arranged around a tiled yard, open to the sky and the abundant sunshine. The yard was bordered by multicolored flowerpots. In summer, when it was too hot indoors, we took our evening meals in this yard and spent our time here until we went to bed. We sometimes slept on the flat roof of the house when the heat indoors was suffocating.

The temple place, with the Dome of the Rock, was a few blocks from our house. For non-Moslems, access to this shrine was restricted to fixed hours on certain days of the week. This did not stop me from going there to play on the grass in the fields all around the shrines. (The Moslem sanctuary, "Haram el Khalil," in Hebron contains the cave of Machpelah. This cave was the burial place of Sarah, Abraham, Isaac, Rebekah, Leah and Joseph, but Jews were not allowed beyond the fifth step of a flight of stairs leading to the inner court. At the fifth step they were allowed to pray, as they did at the Western Wall or "Wailing Wall." Since 1967 Hebron has been occupied by Israel and the Jews have a synagogue in the Haram, or enclosure.)

There were no ready-made clothes and shoes to be bought in department stores. Up to the mid-twenties in Palestine, everything was hand-made. My mother sewed our shirts, pajamas and underwear, as well as our everyday pants and the dresses of my sisters. She also knitted our sweaters during the evening family gatherings.

We had quite a number of family picnics in the outlying parks of the churches, on the saint's day to which each church was dedicated. On these occasions there was a great exodus from Jerusalem, and this large group attended religious services in the church, then later picnicked in the park, enjoying the outdoors and the gifts of Nature.

It was in this way that we visited the Church of the Cross. According to tradition, the cross of Jesus came from a tree that grew in the park surrounding this church. In the church of Katamon is the tomb of St. Simeon. Halfway to Bethlehem is the Convent of St. Elisha. The tomb of Ste. Mary is next to the Gethsemane Garden in the valley of Josaphat. The Mount of Olives has an impressive Russian Church of Ascension with a huge park. It was open to the whole Christian community for picnics on the Day of Ascension. Some families went there on the eve of the feast and spent the night in tents. There were ferris wheels for the children.

We spent our vacations in the Armenian convent in Bethlehem, next to the Grotto of Nativity. I helped Father Khoren celebrate the Armenian Mass near the Grotto. My father and Uncle Artin left early in the moring for Jerusalem and came back late at night. The door to the Church of Nativity is closed at sunset, so when my father and uncle were late, Father Khoren had to let them in through a special underground door in the Armenian convent.

We took hikes from Bethlehem and got to know the surrounding villages very well. We visited the Shepherds' Fields in Beir Sahur. These fields are famous in the idyllic story of Ruth and Boaz. It was also in these fields that the angels brought the happy tidings to the shepherds at the birth of Jesus. Beit Jala is a predominantly Christian village, where the Salisian fathers have their famous Cremisan vineyards and winery. At Jebel Foureidis (Hill of Paradise), known also as Frank Mountain, you can see a great cistern next to the ruins of a fortress. Herod the Great won a victory over Antigonus here. He built a town, called Herodia, and on the summit of the hill a fortress called Herodium. Herod died in Jericho but he was buried here.

Two miles from Bethlehem is El Khadr (St. George). It has a Greek Orthodox Church of St. George, in which the insane were tied to pillars by the so-called "chains of St. George." From here a road leads to an Arab village, Khirbet el Yahud, site of the last resistance of the Jews under Bar Cochba. A little further we came to Qala'at el Burak (Fortress of the Pools), which was built by the Turks for the protection of King Solomon's Pools. Josephus Flavius writes that King Solomon came here to enjoy the gardens. Herod the Great channeled water from here by aqueduct to Herodium.

We also visited my aunt, Soeur Justine, at the St. Joseph's convent. We enjoyed our Bethlehem vacations very much.

On July 11, 1927 we had an earthquake in Palestine. It destroyed many old houses in Nablus, Jaffa and Jerusalem. As a result we spent a few weeks in tents in a large park across from the Armenian convent of St. James on Mt. Zion. We had to leave the old house and move to Haret el Sharaf, "The Honor Quarter," in the Armenian Quarter, a two-minute walk from King David's Tower.

In 1929 increasing opposition to Jewish immigration led to the killing of Jews in Jerusalem and Hebron by Arabs. At this time I was standing across from the King David's Tower when we saw a British police officer leading an Arab, who was under arrest, toward police headquarters. The Superintendent of Police was coming out of the building at that moment. When he saw them, he ordered the police officer to release the Arab and give him back his sword, which the officer had confiscated. My father and uncle, who were watching with me, were flabbergasted to see the freed Arab run off, brandishing his sword and chanting patriotic slogans.

Sometimes the British seemed to favor Jewish interests, sometimes those of the Arabs. Nobody could understand the British policy in Palestine.

Greengrocer market in the Old City of Jerusalem

Mother Hanum, wearing traditional Armenian dress with her first two sons, Joseph and Jacob.

Narrow lane in the Old City of Jerusalem.

Covered market in the Old City of Jerusalem.

Uncle Artin with an Armenian friend wearing Arab headgear (Kafieh) with their Enfield rifles.

The Greek Orthodox Belfry at the entrance of the Church of the Holy Sepulchre.

Holy Shrines of Jerusalem

When I was a sophomore in high school, we lived in a street called "Haret El Sinsilah" — the Street of Chain — in the old city of Jerusalem. Its name came from a chain of arches erected between the houses that led to "Bab El Sinsilah" (the Gate of Chain), the main gate leading to the Temple of Solomon area. This area is sacred to the three monotheistic religions, Christianity, Judaism, and Islam. The gate leads directly to the Dome of the Rock. The building is a mosque, or place of worship, for the Moslem faith.

At the front of the mosque is a porch with seven arches that correspond to the mosque's seven aisles. The rock in the Dome of the Rock is traditionally believed to be the place where Abraham tied the hands of his son Isaac and was preparing to sacrifice him in obedience to the Lord's command, when the voice of an angel said, "Abraham! Abraham! Spare the child. God is convinced of your faith." Abraham looked around him; he saw a ram in the thicket. The angel commanded him to take this ram and sacrifice it in his son's place.

This rock is also venerated by the Moslems, because their prophet Mohammed was conveyed to it from Al Ka'abah, holy shrine of Mecca, by the mysterious winged steed El Borak, accompanied by the Angel Gabriel. Here Mohammed prayed in memory of Abraham, father of monotheism. Afterward El Borak carried him to the seventh heaven. The Moslem custodian shows travelers the imprint of El Borak's hoof on the rock. The Haj, or holy pilgrimage, that Moslems are urged to undertake at least once in their lifetime to the Al Ka'abah shrine in Arabia, is incomplete unless they also visit and pray at this mosque.

The Dome of the Rock is sometimes erroneously called the Mosque of Omar. The real Mosque of Omar is situated across the Holy Sepulchre compound in the Christian Quarter of the old city of Jerusalem. Within the compound are Mount Calvary, scene of the Crucifixion, and the Tomb of the Savior, as well as other holy shrines.

After the Arabs conquered Jerusalem in 638 A.D., Omar Ibn Al-Khattab, the second caliph (supreme chief of Islam), whose impartiality is universally acknowledged, visited the Holy City. He was escorted by a Greek Orthodox priest on a tour of the Holy

Sepulchre. When noon was near, Omar said that he had to leave to say his prayers, as is required of every Moslem. The priest offered to retire and grant him privacy. Omar replied, "I must refuse your kind offer, because it will bring the Christians trouble if I accept. My followers will stake a claim to this area in memory of my having said my noon prayers here." He went out to perform his devotions across the street. Later the Moslems did build a shrine there, calling it the Mosque of Omar. Visitors descending the stairs from the Christian quarter on their way to the Holy Sepulchre cannot miss the sign, "Mosque of Omar," at the entrance to this Moslem shrine.

Up to the time of Omar's visit, Jews were still not permitted to enter the city of Jerusalem, except on the 9th day of Av. in the Jewish calendar. The 9th of Av. was the date on which both temples were destroyed, though in different years. The one built by Solomon was destroyed by the Chaldeans under Nebuchadnezzar in 587 B.C., when the Jews were carried into captivity; the second temple, built by Herod, was destroyed by the Romans in 70 A.D.

On the occasion of Omar's visit, the Jews petitioned him to allow two hundred Jewish families to live in the Holy City. He compromised, ordering that seventy Jewish families be allowed to settle in Jerusalem.

The same Street of Chain leads to the Wailing Wall. It is the only part of the temple that survived the destruction of the last temple. Because it is on the western side, it is also called the Western Wall. Moslems call it Al-Burak (El Borak) because Mohammed's winged steed was tethered to the wall while Mohammed prayed.

Some Jews are offended by the name "Wailing Wall." This name is derived from the actions of the Jews who come to the wall and knock their heads against it, sometimes until they draw blood; they cry, wail, and lament in repentance for the sins of their ancestors, and ask the forgiveness of Jehovah and his aid in recovering the temple area. Large crowds used to come to Jerusalem on Tisha B'Av., the ninth day of the Jewish month of Av., enter the city at Jaffa Gate, and continue through the old city Souk, or market, and the Street of Chain to the Wailing Wall.

My bedroom was at the top of one of the arches, with windows on both sides of the street, and I used to sit on the windowsill watching the multitudes of Jews, singing, chanting, and dancing as they made their way down the Street of Chain to the Wailing Wall. Besides the Tisha B'Av., they also visited the

Wailing Wall on Simchath Torah, the feast of rejoicing in honor of the Torah, and also on Yom Kippur, the Day of Atonement on which God balances his people's good deeds against their bad ones. This took place in the late 'twenties and early 'thirties under the British Mandate in Palestine. Nobody interfered with the various forms of worship practiced by the different religions.

Though we lived in a Moslem quarter, the neighbors on the east side of our house were a Sephardic Jewish family, and our neighbors to the west were Ashkenazi Jews. They were very religious. Contrary to the present situation in Israel, the great majority of Jews living in the Holy Land then practiced their religion. Early on many mornings, or deep in the night, our peace was disturbed by the loud religious chants of the cantors either on our eastern or our western side. They also practiced blowing the Shofar, or ram's horn. It could have been coincidence, but whenever the Sephardim practiced on their ram's horn, the Ashkenazim seemed to join in. When this happened, my mother would say, "Here we go again! The East is trying to outblow the West, or vice versa."

Once while I was trying to memorize a poem of the famous Arab poet Al Maari, there suddenly arose the usual competition of our Sephardic and Ashkenazi neighbors. Since it was midday, the voice of the Muezzin was heard as well, calling the faithful to prayer from a nearby minaret. Crowning all this noise, the bells of the Holy Sepulchre of the Greek Orthodox Church were heard loud and clear, announcing the entry of the Greek Orthodox Patriarch into the Holy Sepulchre.

I thought to myself, "This is very appropriate to the poem I was reading!" It can be translated as follows: "There rose a commotion in Jerusalem between Mohammed and the Messiah. The latter was drumming on a cooking pot and the former shouting on a minaret, each trying to extol his religion. I wish I knew which of them is right."

A piece of the stone that covered the tomb of the Savior, which was moved by the angel.

The walled off "Golden Gate" of the Old City near the temple area. It shall be opened on the day of Last Judgment.

Damascus Gate of the Old City of Jerusalem.

The Mount of Olives with Bethany in the background (on the right).

The Valley of Josaphat, the Mount of Olives in the background and the Garden of Gethsemane in the foreground.

Jewish worshipers at the Wailing or Western Wall. Only remnant of Solomon's Temple.

The Dome of the Rock.

Franciscan friars on the Way of the Cross, on the way to the Church of the Holy
Sepulchre.

Entrance to the Church of St. James, in the Armenian quarter of Jerusalem, decorated with Armenian style ceramic tile.

The Orfali family (Mother, Father, five brothers and two sisters) during the 1930s with Aunt Justine, (of the Convent of St. Joseph).

Life in Palestine under the British Mandate

After December 11, 1917, a proclamation, read in seven languages on the platform at the entrance to the citadel "David's Tower," declared peace and brotherly love. Jerusalem was also placed under martial law. The British expected trouble; in the Balfour Declaration, they had promised the establishment of a national home for the Jewish people in Palestine. At the same time King Hussein of El Hejaz was to receive the crown of a united Arab world, including Palestine in compensation for his aid in the Arab revolt against Turkey. Great Britain was given control of Palestine as a Mandatory Power on July 1, 1926. The military administration was replaced by a civil government, and Sir Herbert Samuel, an English Jew, was appointed the first High Commissioner. Consequently, riots broke out in Jaffa on May 1, 1921, which led to racial strife. It kept erupting in incidents in various parts of the country. On August 23, 1929, increasing opposition to Jewish immigration led to the killing of some 130 Jerusalem Jews by Arabs in what is known as the Wailing Wall Incident. Again, at the end of 1933, there were bloody protests against the government for allowing large-scale immigration to Jews fleeing from Hitler's persecution. The years 1938–1939 saw open warfare between the Arabs and the government, and the country was in a state of disturbance.

Internal strife ceased at the outbreak of World War II. Toward the end of the war the troubles began again, coming this time from the Jewish population. Political pressure, illegal immigration, underground organizations (Hagana, Irqun Znai Leumi, Stern Gang) brought in the United States. As a result, on November 29, 1947, the United Nations General Assembly proclaimed the partition of the country into two independent states, Arab and Jewish, by May 15, 1948. Great Britain was asked to see that the partition was implemented. In reply, the British government declined that responsibility. It stated that the last British forces would leave before midnight of May 14, 1948.

In 1942, Judas Magnes, president of Hebrew University, Jerusalem, along with Martin Buber, the distinguished philosopher, and Henrietta Szold, American-born founder of Hadassah, organized the Ihud, or Union Party, which supported the goal of a binational state in Palestine. The religious fundamentalists of the Agudath Israel opposed the creation of the State of Israel.

In the late 1920s and early 1930s, while growing up in the city of Jerusalem, I attended the Christian Brothers' College. This school was situated just inside the New Gate of the old city of Jerusalem, which was the nearest gateway to the new modern city.

Maybe I should call it "utopia." The Christian Brothers are a Catholic community dedicated to education. This doesn't mean they educated only Catholics at their school. The cosmopolitan student body included Protestants, Greek Orthodox, Russian Orthodox, Armenian Gregorians, Abyssinians, Copts, Jews, Moslems, and members of the Bahai faith.

For example, one of my classmates was the son of the Mayor of Jerusalem, Ragheb Bey Nashashibi. The mayor himself was Mohammedan, but his wife was Jewish. During elections, the Jews of Jerusalem voted for him. They considered his wife a modern-day Esther.

Another classmate was the son of the Turkish consul in Jerusalem. We got on very well, despite the fact that Armenians like myself were supposed to shun Turks because of the massacres of Armenians in Turkey.

The son of the Abyssinian consul was yet another classmate of mine, as was the son of a Greek Orthodox priest. My very best friend was Petia, whose Russian Orthodox family had fled Russia when the Communists took over. They lived in the Russian compound, a great complex of dwellings near the beautiful Russian Orthodox Church in the new city, not far from the New Gate. When he and his family moved away from Jerusalem, my friendship with Tony, a French boy, became stronger, and we spent all our free time together after school.

Looking back, I cannot help feeling deeply as I relive the many happy moments we spent together. We explored the villages and towns around Jerusalem on bicycles, on primitive dirt roads or even narrow footpaths, roaming up the hills and down into deep valleys that may have been traversed for thousands of years by pilgrims on their way to worship in the holy shrines of Jerusalem. Thus we visited Bethlehem, where Christ was born, Hebron, where Abraham and his family were buried; Ramallah, Nablus, the old Schechem, where the descendants of the Samaritans lived for thousands of years, and still live now on and around Mount Geriseem.

We also explored the caves on the way to Jericho, Jericho itself, the Dead Sea, and the Jordan River, Emmaus, where Jesus appeared to his disciples on the third day after the Crucifixion. The Franciscan order built a sanctuary there, surrounded by a lovely garden and a pine forest. This was one of our favorite places. We took every opportunity to visit and enjoy the awesome beauty of nature and to lie under the trees. The delicate rustle of the wind among the leaves was like sweet music in our ears.

We would rise before dawn. Using the morning star as our guide, we reached the first village just at daybreak, in time to catch the village women at the taboun. The taboun is a dome-shaped earthenware oven, filled with small rocks. A fire was lit around the oven to heat the rocks. After the fire had burned out, the women would place thinly rolled dough on the rocks to be baked into bread. The bread looked strange with its rounded indentations from the heated rocks, but it tasted great to two hungry young boys. We ate it with freshly made butter, and sometimes hard-boiled eggs, baked in the same taboun. For desert we had freshly picked grapes, figs, or apricots, depending on the season.

Once when we looked down from the top of a mountain into the valley, we heard the roosters announce the birth of a new day, we listened to the chorus of sheep, lambs, and cows, and watched the smoke rise lazily from the breakfast fires. We spied the first rays of the sun glisten like jewels in the dew on the trees. These were the rewards that lured us out of our warm beds and into the darkness before dawn.

At our school, we all had to learn our subjects in three different languages: French, English, and Arabic. If one spoke an additional language at home, one grew up speaking four languages from childhood on. During our recreation periods at school, we spoke only French in the morning and only English in the afternoon. Arabic was the language used in our daily dealings with people outside school. To enforce the language rules, the school administrator would give one of the students a wooden disk, called a "signal." This student passed it to anyone who did not speak the required language. The signal kept being passed to those who slipped. The last student to receive the disk at the end of recreation had to study a poem or write a theme in the language he had neglected to speak.

After graduation, my classmates played active roles in the governments of their countries, or became business executives, lawyers, or doctors. The most important feature of our education was learning to respect the religious and political affiliations of others.

Orfali family picnic during the Summer of 1940 in Ain Karem, birthplace of St. John the Babtist.

Dikran Orfali (my brother) while sergeant interpreter in the British Army during WWII.

General Sir Edmund Allenby, unlike Kaiser Wilhelm, dismounted his horse and walked into the city of Jerusalem through the Jaffa Gate. He did this to show that he came as a friend and liberator rather than as conqueror.

King Abdullah, surrounded by his entourage, during a visit to the Dome of the Rock.

People of Palestine before the State of Israel

Whenever my friends introduce me, they make a point of mentioning that I was born in Jerusalem. The usual reaction is, "Oh, Israel! How is life over there? When are you going back?" I reply, "The U.S. is my home. I may go back to visit Israel, but I have no desire to stay." People stare incredulously at me, and I have to explain that not everyone who was born or living in Jerusalem before the creation of the State of Israel was a Jew.

There were many separate communities in Jerusalem, each living in its own enclave — the Armenians, the Greeks, the Syriacs, the Germans, the Roman Catholics, the Moslems, and, of course, the Jews. The Jews had two separate communities, the Sephardim and the Ashkenazim. The Sephardim (a word that means "Spanish" in Hebrew) are the descendants of the Jews who fled to North Africa, Egypt, Greece, Turkey, and other countries during the Spanish Inquisition. The Ashkenazim are descended from Jews who lived in Germany in the Middle Ages; when they were discriminated against and mistreated, they fled to Eastern and Western Europe. In Israel, both communities practiced the customs of the countries where they had lived before coming to the Holy Land. Needless to say, they felt alien to their fellow Jews. The Sephardim spoke a language derived from Spanish, mixed with words and expressions picked up in the other countries where they had lived. Likewise, the Ashkenazim spoke a kind of mediæval German, mixed with words from other countries. Each community showed some tolerance toward the other. In fact, each resented the other's customs and way of life. They had two separate Chief Rabbis. There was also a small community of Yemenite Jews, whose ancestors had never left the Arabian Peninsula. They were very gentle people, famous for the filigreed silver jewelry they created. They spoke Arabic and kept a low profile.

Though world Jewry contributed generously to the Jewish Agency to buy land in Palestine, very few Jews felt the urge to emigrate. They considered themselves a part of the culture of whatever country they lived in. The rise of Hitler and Nazism forced the Jews of Europe to seek a haven from persecution, because the Western countries admitted only a token number of immigrants; the others had nowhere to go but the Holy Land.

English, Arabic and Hebrew were official government languages. Before the 1930s very few Jews spoke Hebrew. Correspondence with the British Mandate government was conducted in English, and the city administration in Arabic. I remember an incident related to me by the chief clerk of the Jerusalem Municipality, located in Mamillah Road outside the Jaffa Gate. They received a letter in Hebrew and nobody could read it. They even asked the Jewish merchants near the city hall for help, but nobody could oblige. Finally they found a priest, a Biblical scholar, who agreed to do the translation.

Among the Christian population, there was always an Armenian community in Jerusalem. Their number multiplied with the influx of refugees fleeing the genocide perpetrated by the Turks. Armenia, the first nation to accept the Christian faith, always had strong ties to the Holy Land. The last Armenian kingdom in Cilicia was a faithful ally of the Crusaders. The first two Christian queens of Jerusalem were Armenian princesses. Many other Armenian ladies married into the European nobility. An Armenian brigade, with volunteers from all over the world, fought with the Allies during World War I to liberate the Holy Land from the Turks. Those who fell are buried in the Armenian cemetery of Mount Zion, in a common grave called the Tomb of the Martyrs.

The Armenian Patriarch of Jerusalem is the custodian of one-third of the shrines in the Church of the Holy Sepulchre in Jerusalem and the Church of Nativity in Bethlehem. Most of the Armenians in Jerusalem lived within the compound of the Armenian convent. It is like an independent village. The clergy are responsible for the security, water supply, garbage collection, and so on. Its doors are closed at 9 P.M. daily and do not open until 6 A.M. the next day. The compound has its own holy shrine in the St. James' Cathedral, where the head of St. James, brother of Jesus, is buried in a small chapel. The convent had always housed pilgrims who came to the Holy Land. Its doors were opened to the Armenian refugees from the genocide perpetrated by the Turkish government against its Armenian subjects during and after World War I.

There was also a large number of Armenians in the Armenian quarter, which is just outside the convent walls. I was born in the Armenian quarter of Jerusalem. We spoke Armenian at home. I learned Turkish from the neighbors, Armenian refugees, who spoke only Turkish as is required by law in Turkey. Later, as a teenager at the Christian Brothers' College of Jerusalem, I learned English, French, and Arabic. When I went to work for the C.I.D. (the British Mandate's Criminal Investigation Department), I had to learn Hebrew. This became necessary after the large influx of Jewish immigrants, whose leaders insisted on dealing with the governmental offices only in Hebrew and encouraged their people to do likewise. A substantial number of the newcomers were from Germany and could speak only German. Thus I had to learn their language too. As you can see, at that time people like me became fluent in many languages in the normal course of their lives. This is how I came to speak seven languages while still a young man.

The Greek Patriarch is custodian of one-third of the Holy Shrines. The large Greek population in Jerusalem was divided into two communities. One was made up of immigrants from Greece and their offspring. They spoke only Greek among themselves, but used some crude Arabic in business. The second group were called the Levantines. These were the descendants of Greeks who had lived in countries that were under Greek rule for many centuries in the Middle East. They considered themselves part of the cultures they inhabited, and spoke the native languages. In Palestine they spoke Arabic and even used that language in their prayers. They were fanatical Arab nationalists — even their priests were active in the Arab cause. Dr. George Habash, leader of one of the fighting Palestinian groups (who are called terrorists), belongs to this community. Their only tie with the other Greeks is that they all belong to the Greek Orthodox Church.

The Roman Catholic Patriarch is custodian of one-third of the Holy Shrines. The Roman Catholics were known as Latins because they used Latin in their liturgy. This custom was changed after Vatican II, as decreed by the universally beloved John XXIII. During my last visit to Israel some years ago, I witnessed a Mass being celebrated in Arabic by an Italian Franciscan priest in the parish of St. Savior of the Old City, Jerusalem, and another Mass celebrated in Hebrew by an Irish priest in the convent of the Ratisbonne fathers in the New City of Jerusalem.

The Latin community comprised the diplomats representing the Catholic nations — such as France, Spain, Italy, Austria, and the Latin American countries — as well as the Catholic diplomats of non-Catholic nations such as the United States, England, Germany, and so on. Also represented were most of the Catholic religious orders, such as the Benedictines, who had two different convents (one German, the other French), the Salizians, the Trappists, the Christian Brothers, the Sisters of St. Joseph, the Sisters of Zion, and the Sisters of Charity, among others.

The members of the local Latin community were the descendants of Catholics of different nationalities who had come as pilgrims and decided to continue living in Jerusalem. Others were descendants of Crusaders who had married local women. Some were artisans who were brought over by the various religious orders when their convents were being built, and decided not to return to their native countries.

Most of the local Latin citizens had European names, such as Norman, Lorenz, Meo, Sabella, Albina, and so on. They had lost their original nationalities with the passage of time and traveled with Palestinian passports issued by the British authorities. At home they spoke French, Spanish, Italian, and so on. These people suffered when the State of Israel was created. They were treated as Arabs even though neither their language nor their culture was Arabic. A small number of Latins did speak Arabic and were active in the Arab cause. Some were arrested by the Israelis when they took over the new city of Jerusalem in 1948, and were kept in concentration camps under primitive conditions. Later, with the aid of the Red Cross, they were allowed to cross over to the old city. Among those arrested was Maestro Agustin Lama, director of the Latin community's choir and well-known composer of religious music.

Other small Christian communities, the Syriacs, the Chaldeans, and the various Protestant churches, were represented as well in Jerusalem. They mostly kept to themselves.

A large group of Germans, the German Templars, lived in the German colony of Jerusalem. They were businessmen and skilled technicians. There were other German colonies in the south and in Haifa, whose ancestors had emigrated to the Holy Land many generations before. The Moslem community was, of course, the largest. It too was divided into many groups of different origins — the Arabs, the Turks, the Pakistanis, the Moroccans, the Bukharians, the Persians, and so on.

This, in a nutshell, is the variety of people who lived in the Holy Land. Since the various religious communities were competing for students, Palestinians were blessed with unparalleled opportunities for education.

Christmas in Bethlehem

Every December, the world prepares to celebrate an event which occurred twenty centuries ago in Bethlehem, a small town of Judea — the birth of the greatest innovator of all time.

Whether or not one believes Jesus of Nazareth is the Messiah promised in the Old Testament, no one can help recognizing that he was the Prince of Peace. Nobody can deny that his teachings of love and charity, if literally practiced, would transform this valley of turmoil and suffering into the Promised Land of our dreams.

Unfortunately, the so-called leaders and teachers of the philosophy of Jesus interpret it wrongly. Blinded by their own self-importance, they make no effort to understand his very plain teachings, which he expressed simply when he said, "Love thy neighbor as thyself." Peace and happiness will come only when people stop thinking, "What's in it for me?" before they plunge into a project. They should rather ask, "Would it benefit everybody?"

Having said what lies heavily on my heart, I will proceed to my main topic, which is the way Christmas is celebrated in the birthplace of Jesus Christ.

On the morning of December 24, the Patriarch, or Archbishop of Jerusalem of the Roman Catholic Church, leaves the Archdiocese Seat of Jerusalem to make his way to Bethlehem. His limousine is preceded and surrounded by an honor guard of security forces on horseback. In ancient times, he and his retinue traveled in horsedrawn carriages. He is met by Catholic notables and by the highest-ranking government officers — who nowadays are Israelites — near Rachel's Tomb. This marks the city boundary of Bethlehem, where he is greeted and welcomed.

The whole party then proceeds to the Manger Square in Bethlehem. The Square is a large open plaza leading to the Church of Nativity, which was built by Ste. Helena, mother of King Constantine, in the Third Century A.D. Its original structure is the oldest existing Christian church. It has survived many non-Christian invaders. According to tradition, when the Persian conquerors attempted to destroy it, they were chased away by hordes of snakes. (The Persian conquerors claimed that when their warriors entered the Church of Nativity, they saw a painting of the Adoration of the Magi. When they saw Persian wise men in the picture, they withdrew in respect instead of destroying the church.)

The Mayor and the City Council of Bethlehem, together with members of the clergy, the boy scouts, musical bands, and the general public, receive the Patriarch at the Manger Square. They extend him the honor due his rank, after which he enters the church in a religious procession, preceded by various choruses singing Christmas songs.

Pilgrims and tourists from all over the world flood Bethlehem on this occasion. Some come to pay their respects, others merely to satisfy their curiosity.

Bethlehem has no large hotels. This is a typical reminder of the time of Christ's birth, when Joseph and Mary had to sleep in one of the caves or grottos near Bethlehem. Most tourists and other visitors stay in Jerusalem, which is five miles away, and visit Bethlehem by cab or bus. The Franciscan Friars, who are the Custodians of the Holy Land, maintain a small inn called the Casa Nova where they accommodate the Patriarch and visiting clergy.

Incidentally, the Greek Orthodox Christians celebrate their Christmas one week after December 25. The Armenians celebrate it on January 18. These three denominations share equally the Church of Nativity. Their Patriarchs are given the same courteous receptions and honors when they come to Bethlehem on their respective Christmas Eves.

The midnight mass is celebrated by the Catholics in the Church of Ste. Catherine, from which it is broadcast to the world. Its climax is the time of birth, which is announced by the church bells and the Hallelujahs. Then the "Bambino" representing the infant Jesus is carried by the Patriarch, in a procession singing Christmas carols, to the Manger where it is placed.

It is only fair to mention that many different Protestant communities are also present to celebrate the birth of the Savior. There was a time when the Church was divided among the Christian denominations and there were no Protestants. That is why they meet in groups in the Manger Square or in the shepherd's field where they conduct their services.

Feast of the Prophet Nebi Musa

In the Twelfth Century, the Christian kingdom in the Holy Land, created by the Crusaders, had found a "modus vivendi," a way of living peacefully with its neighbors. The star of Saladin was rising because of his shrewd compromises with potential opponents and his friendship with the neighboring Christian rulers.

At about this time, the restless offspring of the European nobility swarmed into the Middle East. They led gangs of desperadoes who were motivated not by Christian zeal but by the excitement of a life of adventure. They committed highway robberies. Without differentiating between Christians and Moslems, they raided the cities, looting and massacring the inhabitants.

In 1187, a four-year truce with Saladin's Christian neighbors was broken by the brilliant brigand Raynalt of Chatillon. Saladin, who was expecting trouble from the Turks in the north, decided to get rid of this thorn in his side for good. He waged a full-scale war against the Christians. After defeating them, he occupied the Holy City of Jerusalem. He made an impartial treaty with his conquered foes. He gave unlimited pilgrimage rights, and free access with protection to the holy places, to all the Christian world.

Because of his unsavory experiences in the past, he had misgivings about the pilgrims' future behavior during the Easter holidays. Their number would exceed by far that of the local Moslems of Jerusalem. He therefore created a Moslem holiday to honor the prophet Moses. (The Moslems consider Moses their kin because his wife was the daughter of Jethro, the Midianite who introduced him to monotheism in the Sinai.)

Moses was not permitted to enter the Promised Land because he had disobeyed the orders of Jehovah. Instead he was allowed to get a glimpse of the country from the top of Mount Nebo, east of the Jordan River.

Saladin perfected a scheme whereby the Moslems from the neighboring towns and villages were concentrated in Jerusalem during Easter week. They came to Jerusalem in well-organized processions, carrying victory banners and shouting religious and national slogans on their way to the Mosque of El Aksa to pray. They exhibited their fencing, wrestling, and other martial skills in the area of the Temple of Solomon, where they camped overnight. The next day they continued their pilgrimage to a mountain near the Dead Sea where Moslems believe is the tomb of the prophet Moses, known as "El Nebi Musa." This coincided with the Palm Sunday celebration of the Christians. After spending a week in Nebi Musa, the celebrants returned to Jerusalem by Easter Sunday. There, they were ready for any trouble created by Christian pilgrims. These Nebi Musa pilgrimages continued until the end of the British Mandate over Palestine in 1947.

This time of the year made a very vivid impression on me in my childhood. For weeks in my father's candy factory, the workers would make nothing but halvah, a confection made with sesame butter. They stacked the halvah in two-pound packages. The Arab villagers, on their way back home, would buy from ten to fifteen packages each, to bring as presents from the big city for their friends and relatives.

The Bedouins

Bedouins are Arabs, but not all Arabs are Bedouins. Bedouins are nomads. Like American Indians, they are considered children of nature. They enjoy the freedom of the desert spaces, and savor the awesome nights of crystal-clear, star-dotted skies. Their continuous exposure to nature has convinced them that there can be only one Supreme Master of the Universe, who has engineered the perfect timing and the smooth running of the whole thing.

Abraham, himself a nomad chief, not only practiced monotheism but made its adoption mandatory for his followers.

Moses, after he fled into the Sinai Desert from Egypt, was introduced to monotheism by his father-in-law Jethro. Jethro was a nomad Midianite sheik, most probably a descendent of Ishmael, the firstborn son of Abraham and the maiden Hagar. According to law, a barren wife could present her maid to the husband and acknowledge the resulting children as her own, so that he would have heirs. This happened when Sarah presented her maid Hagar to Abraham, and later when Rachel and Leah presented theirs to Jacob. The descendants of Jacob's children by the maid are among the twelve tribes of Israel. However, after Isaac was born to Sarah, she made Abraham banish Hagar and her son Ishmael to the desert. They were picked up and adopted by Bedouins. Eventually Ishmael became the prolific leader of a prosperous Bedouin tribe.

Abraham is said to have been a very generous host. He was lonely when he had no guests. He would retire to his tent and brood in solitude, but would perk up upon hearing his scouts announce that they had spotted travelers approaching from the distant horizon. He would immediately order arrangements to welcome the weary guests.

This custom is still practiced by the desert Bedouins of today. There is little water in the area where the Bedouins pitch their tents, but the head of the family makes sure a traveler is provided with enough. His own men help the newcomer to clean up by pouring water on his hands and feet, since there is no modern piping system.

After the ablutions and a short rest, the traveler is entertained with the best meal his host can provide. The main dish is usually a big tray of rice and chunks of lamb swimming in broth. This is covered with very thin round bread, called pita, which looks like a giant pancake. The tray is placed in the center of the tent where the guests are assembled. Each one breaks off a piece of the bread, digs into the rice with his fingers, forms a small ball and sticks it into his mouth. Yogurt and buttermilk are served with the meal. Loud burps, both during the feasting and afterward, are the approved sounds of appreciation for a good meal.

As a special honor to a guest, the host fishes out an especially tender morsel of meat with his fingers from the tray and offers it to him. The guest, of course, receives it with his own fingers. After asking Allah to multiply by a hundredfold the wealth of his host and bless him with good health, happiness, and a limitless number of strong male children, he consumes the gift. The host responds with fitting compliments. These exchanges continue during and after the serving of coffee. Only afterward is it time to discuss the purpose of the visit.

As a general rule, when a visitor reaches an encampment, he is welcomed and led to the tent of the head of the family or sheik, which means "venerable old man" in Arabic. After the greetings, the sheik offers the newcomer a cup of sweet coffee.

There are no tables or chairs in the tents. The floor is covered with carpeting. People sit on thick rugs on the floor, leaning on pillows made of saddlebags. The sheik sits facing the entrance to the tent. Before him stands a charcoal stove holding two pots, the large one filled with sweet coffee, and the smaller one containing bitter coffee. Continuous brewing makes the coffee thick and strong. The visitor is offered the bitter brew first. He consumes it with a loud sucking noise to show his appreciation. When he has won his host's confidence, the latter offers him a second cup containing a few drops of the sweet coffee from the large pot. This means that the visitor is accepted as a friend and, as such, is invited to share the sweet and bitter things in life together with his host.

Coffee was known and consumed by the Arab and Middle Eastern peoples long before it was introduced to the Western world by the Turks. A legend attributes its discovery to a shepherd boy. He noticed that whenever his goats ate the fruits of a certain tree, they became highstrung and behaved strangely. They jumped and ran about in circles as if performing some ritual dance. His curiosity drove him to taste the fruit himself. He was rewarded with a light-headed feeling and a pleasant sensation. Certain coffee beans are known by the name of Mocha, which refers to Mecca, the holy city of Islam in Arabia.

The Bedouins have many customs or codes of ethics that seem strange to Westerners. For example, they are tremendously vengeful. However, if the killer of a member of a tribe succeeds in entering the sheik's tent and asking for mercy, he is granted refuge and protection for twenty-four hours. He is then allowed to get under way, and only after he has escaped is he pursued for revenge.

Camels are a vital element of the Bedouins' nomadic life. Camels can go for days without water. They are called the "ships of the desert" because they can carry heavy loads for long distances in arid climates. Camels also supply milk and meat. Their hair is spun into carpets and tents, and their hide used to make leather.

The Bedouins are also skilled horsemen. Their thoroughbred Arabian horses are treated like members of the family. In modern Israel, where their movements are restricted for security reasons, they now have pick-up trucks instead of camels and horses parked outside their tents or mud houses.

In the Arab countries, young Bedouins who leave the nomadic life are offered the best education available anywhere in the world. It is financed by the government with oil revenues.

Jordan does not have oil. Yet it is fast becoming a very pleasant oasis with its modern hotels, night clubs, international restaurants, modern roads, and sumptuous stone buildings. It has a moderate climate, no crime problem, and an efficient police force. Mugging is unheard of. Jordan is a resort where the oil-wealthy sheiks flock in with their families and spend lavishly.

A large portion of the well-disciplined Jordanian army is composed of Bedouins. Their trustworthiness and complete dedication to the throne make them the backbone of the kingdom of Jordan.

The following story may illustrate the character and behavior pattern of the Bedouins: My brothers have a macaroni factory in Amman, Jordan. They are also the sole agents for Agfa, the German equivalent of Eastman Kodak. They had distribution centers on the West Bank of the Jordan. After the Six Day War in 1967, the Israeli government froze all the assets of Jordanian businessmen in the newly occupied West Bank. This created a financial crisis for my brothers, since the banks kept pressuring them to pay their overdue bills.

At about this time, a Bedouin sheik who had befriended my brothers came to visit. Sensing the gloomy atmosphere, he inquired as to its cause. On being told about the situation he immediately left, saying that he had an urgent matter to settle, but would be back shortly.

When he reappeared he was carrying a shopping bag, which he presented to my brother Leon, saying, "This may come in handy." Leon accepted it and thanked him without knowing what was in the bag. He placed it nonchalantly in a corner next to where he sat. As prescribed by the etiquette of the land, he did not try to see its contents. Soon afterward, his Bedouin friend excused himself and left the shop. When the bag was opened, my brothers were amazed to find a pile of banknotes totaling $150,000. Enclosed was an apologetic note explaining that this was all the sheik had available at the moment, but that he would try to get more if it was needed.

What a windfall! Imagine, no promissory note, no collateral, not even the traditional handshake that normally seals a business transaction with Bedouins.

We should now be better able to understand the behavior of the Saudis toward America, which they consider their friend. Their king is a Bedouin sheik.

Bedouin woman at the ancient ruins in Petra.

Young Bedouin man at the ancient ruins in Petra.

Mother Hanum and her sisters wearing traditional Bedouin clothes for Carnival (Mardi Gras).

An Angry Old Man

In the Moslem countries a woman may not appear in public without a veil covering her face and a long robe covering her body down to the ankles. At home she is forbidden to show herself to any male visitor except members of her immediate family. Whenever a male stranger, such as a plumber or an electrician, has some business in a house, he must be accompanied by a male member of the family or make an appointment in advance and confine his movements to the place where his services are needed. Before entering the house, he knocks at the door and shouts three times, "O, Allah! O Shelterer!" He is free to enter after he hears from the oldest lady of the house that the coast is clear.

I knew a Moslem grandfather who built a prosperous brassware business, selling mostly to tourists in the old city of Jerusalem. He had retired and his three sons ran the business, but he still went early each morning to the shop and came back home late in the afternoon after closing time. He ate lunch in the shop with his sons. It was prepared at home and sent over at noon with one of the children. Everyone in the family lived together in a big house with a courtyard in the middle. Each couple, with their children, lived in a separate flat in the house.

This old man was very fanatical and interpreted the Koran, the holy book of the Moslems, with extreme severity. Whenever he saw a Moslem woman whose veil was not entirely opaque, or one whose robe had shrunk a few inches while it was washed, he would berate her loudly and call her all kinds of names. His unfortunate victim would flee from him, running as fast as she could. His neighbors, who witnessed these scenes, disliked his excessive zeal, but his sharp tongue frightened them into silence.

One day after eating lunch he grew very tired. His sons heard his complaints and urged him to go home and rest. He reluctantly agreed. One of the sons offered to accompany him, but he angrily refused, and off he went.

Since he was entering his own house, he did not need to give the warning signal. He almost suffered a stroke when he came into the courtyard. His favorite granddaughter stood nearly naked in a transparent nightgown, which she modeled suggestively for the other women. A Jewish salesman, his wares spread about him, was clearly enjoying the scene.

Uttering unprintable words, the grandfather rushed to his room, got his gun, and aimed it at the salesman. Before he could pull the trigger, his wife intervened, imploring him to calm down. When his temper had cooled a bit, he said, "Stupid woman, you are ruining my reputation and making a laughing stock of me! How can I ever preach about our religious customs and rules to others after what you have done to me today?"

His favorite granddaughter responded, "But Grandpa, he is a Jew, not a Moslem."

The grandfather thought a moment. Then he said, "All right! If that's the way it seems to you, I'll prove that even if he's Jewish, he's still male." Holding the salesman at gunpoint, he threatened to kill him unless he took off all his clothing. The poor fellow kneeled and pleaded, promising never again to enter a Moslem house. The women also wailed and pleaded with the old man, but he adamantly kept his gun trained on the salesman, threatening him ever more loudly, until his victim was stark naked.

The women shrieked and turned away their faces. But the old man said, "You'd better look! Is there any difference between a Moslem male and a Jewish male? The Jews are our cousins. Had not the barren Sarah prevailed upon the weakling Abraham to send away our grandmother Hagar with his firstborn son Ishmael, we would be God's chosen people instead of the descendants of Isaac." While the old man was busy preaching at his women, the salesman quickly put on his clothes, gathered his wares, and stole away.

The newlyweds in their first home.

How I Met My Wife Stephanie

My wife Stephanie was born into a German Jewish family in Nurnberg, Germany. While studying chemistry, she was forced to leave on account of the political situation when Hitler and his gang took over. She came to Palestine, where she joined a girls' Agro school in Affuleh. The intense heat and humidity affected her health. Her asthma got worse in that atmosphere. On her doctor's advice, she moved to Jerusalem, which is on a plateau where the air is dry and clear.

I met Stephanie in the summer of 1935 in the new city of Jerusalem, at the Monastery of the Cross. As we talked, we found we shared many common interests and decided to meet again the next day in a café. We enjoyed each other's companionship and conversation on diverse subjects. Over two hours had passed when we had to leave because of previous commitments. I asked for the bill, and was embarrassed when Stephanie offered to pay her share. I had heard of going "Dutch treat," but it had never occurred to me that I would be faced with such a situation myself. I explained gently to her that she should not be offended, but it was the custom in our milieu for a gentleman escorting a lady to pay the bill.

Before separating, we decided to take a course in the Hebrew language, which was offered for adults on Thursday nights at seven. So we met every Thursday at the class, and afterward we would go to an outdoor café for a snack. At first, we talked about the course and the lesson to be prepared for the following week, but soon we began to speak of more personal matters. By the end of the course we were sharing glimpses of our backgrounds and our lives.

We began to meet outside of class. We took trips together to villages around Jerusalem and to the suburbs. Our discussions of diverse cultural subjects continued, and we began to cherish each other's companionship. We had a very dear platonic friendship. We realized we had better cut it short before it developed into something more intimate. Stephanie soon left Jerusalem.

Ten days after her departure, I was at work at police headquarters. At about noon the office messenger came to tell me a lady was asking for me at the gate. I looked out of my second-story window and saw Stephanie waving to me. We continued to meet regularly for a long time, until we fell deeply in love.

Our problems began when we decided to get married. It was almost impossible to have a mixed marriage between a Jew and a Christian performed in Palestine, where there is no such thing as a civil ceremony. One of the parties would have to convert to the faith of the other; then a religious ceremony would take place. However, I had been baptized in the Roman Catholic faith, which had a "hush-hush" edict requiring the church to perform a mixed marriage not at the altar, but in the sacristy. The non-Catholic party had to swear to bring up the children as Catholics.

The old parish priest who had baptized me flatly refused to marry us. We went to see the Patriarch Archbishop of Jerusalem. He interviewed each of us separately, several times. At our last meeting with him, he told us he had given the parish priest a week to perform the ceremony, and that if it had not been done in that time, the Patriarch Archbishop would perform it himself. The parish priest did perform the ceremony, in the sacristy of the St. Savior Parish Church in Jerusalem.

Our first son, George Michael, was born on September 30, 1940, our daughter Gabrielle Marie on September 28, 1942, and our son Joseph Sebastian on August 26. They were baptized in the Armenian Catholic Church in Jerusalem. Our fourth child, John Paul, was born and baptized in 1951 in the Roman Catholic parish church in Bethlehem.

There are ups and downs in every marriage. We had our share of good luck, sometimes against very strong odds. We had our share of friends who tried to influence our reactions against each other's minor failings. We had promised each other to stick together no matter what, even when others tried to create storms in our lives. It wasn't easy, and we sometimes felt we needed superhuman power to withstand the assaults of well-meaning busybodies.

We succeeded, though. We will soon be celebrating our golden wedding anniversary. We are now retired and have reached the end of the tunnel, where we are greeted not only by the proverbial light, but by bright sunshine. Our four children have all graduated from college, each successful in his or her career and happily married. We are proud of what we have accomplished in our life together.

Father Curtin's Black Suit

My family lived in Jerusalem, Palestine, during World War II when it was still under British Mandate.

We belonged to a Catholic social club called "The Sword of the Spirit." It met every Thursday night. English-speaking servicemen, visiting the Holy Land on furlough from units stationed in Africa and Europe, were happy to join us in a place that offered them genuine sympathy and understanding in a warm civilian atmosphere. It was a kind of home away from home for them.

Our meetings and activities took place on premises provided by the Catholic Archdiocese of Jerusalem, under the guidance of Father Curtin, an Irish priest born in England. He made his presence as unobtrusive as possible. Father Curtin belonged to a religious order, the "Fathers of Zion," created by a German Jew from Ratisbone (or Regensburg), who became a priest after adopting the Catholic faith. The aim of the order is to convert the Jews to Catholicism. They had a large convent, where they ran a free technical school, right in the center of the Jewish Quarter in the new city of Jerusalem.

The Sword of the Spirit offered the usual activities: here a serviceman could relax, write letters, listen to music, and so on. In addition, he had the opportunity to meet local people who invited him to their homes and alleviated, at least for a while, his feelings of loneliness and sometimes despair.

Father Curtin deserves praise for his contributions and his unselfish dedication to making everyone feel at ease and take part in the activities. Unlike other priests I knew, he drank with us, played poker with us, told jokes, and sang popular songs. He also counseled us and performed his religious duties when necessary. It was a delight to have him around. We enjoyed his practical outlook on life, and especially his sense of humor.

Our house was the scene of many parties at which dinner was served to young men and women who missed a home-cooked dinner in a family atmosphere. We lost count of the many birthday cakes and the gallons of coffee and tea that Stephanie, my wife, prepared on such occasions.

We received numerous letters of gratitude from these people. They wrote to us for many years, even after they were discharged from the armed forces and were back at home. In addition to the social gatherings, we took them on short excursions. We went with them to Bethlehem and showed them the Grotto of Nativity where Jesus was born and the Manger where the infant was placed after his birth. We visited an adjacent cave where St. Jerome lived while translating the Bible into Latin and was visited by lions who befriended him. We also saw the field where the angels brought the happy tidings of the Savior's birth to the assembled shepherds.

In Jerusalem we showed them the palace of Caiphas, the Jewish High Priest, where Jesus was tried by the Sanhedrin and condemned to die. We took them to the Garden of Gethsemane, scene of his last agony, and from there climbed the Mount of Olives to where Jesus stood before ascending to heaven.

We reserved this spot for our last stop, to crown a day full of deep emotions, for this reason: The Mount of Olives faces Mount Moriah, where the Temple of Solomon was built. On this site a large mosque, called the Dome of the Rock, now encompasses the rock on which Abraham, in obedience to God's command, prepared to sacrifice his son Isaac. (This holy shrine is also venerated by the Moslems as the place from which the prophet Mohammed ascended to heaven on his horse El Borak, after praying here.) We timed our arrival so that we would be facing the Temple area at sunset, mesmerized by the exhilarating colors of the sun as it glittered behind the gold-plated dome with the whole golden city around it. We felt a sudden deep hush descending upon the earth. Even the birds stopped twittering while the sun sank in a pool of fire. In Jerusalem, the sun disappears quickly below the horizon as if in sudden death. It is quite unlike the slow lingering nightfall of this country.

These glorious excursions were ended, along with the meetings of the Sword of the Spirit, when the peace of the Holy Land was shattered at the end of World War II. The Jews felt betrayed by Britain when that nation refused to open the gates of Palestine to homeless refugees from the concentration camps.

Before condemning the British government, let us review the situation. The British had issued a declaration, through their Foreign Secretary Lord Arthur James Balfour, on November 2, 1917. It said:

"His Majesty's government view with favor the establishment in Palestine of a national home of the Jewish people and will use their best endeavor to facilitate the achievement of this object, it being clearly understood that nothing shall be done which may prejudice the civil and religious rights of the existing non-Jewish communities in Palestine, or the rights and political status enjoyed by Jews in any other country."

The same government had previously made promises, which conflicted with the Balfour declaration, to Sharif Hussein Ibn Ali of Hijaz in Arabia, great-grandfather of the present king of Jordan. The legendary Colonel Lawrence of Arabia, author of *The Seven Pillars of Wisdom*, mediated the agreement. It was made in 1916 and, in accordance with Bedouin customs, was sealed only with a handshake. At that time the Bedouin king agreed to incite the Arab revolt against the Ottoman Empire. Lawrence's friends and comrades-in-arms were the princes Faisal, Ali, and Abdullah, sons of King Hussein. Their famous attacks on the Hijaz railways, which carried ammunition and badly-needed supplies and reinforcements to the front in World War I, brought defeat to the forces of the German-Ottoman axis in the Middle East.

Concurrently with the promises made to the Jewish and Arab peoples, the British and French, on May 9, 1916, entered into a clandestine treaty with the intention of carving up the region. This treaty, called Sykes-Picot after the negotiators, ignored both the Jewish aspirations and Sharif Hussein's ambitions.

After World War II, none of the Western nations was willing to accept a large number of former concentration camp inmates. The non-Jewish communities in Palestine opposed a large-scale influx of Jewish immigrants. They cited the Balfour Declaration, though they had never recognized it. A large influx of Jews would prejudice their civil and religious rights. The British gave this as their reason for refusing to allow large-scale Jewish immigration.

This enraged the Jewish extremist groups, who unleashed full-scale terrorist activities against anything British. They shot poor innocent Tommies (a name given to British soldiers) in their sleep in furlough camp tents. They blew up the British headquarters at the King David Hotel in Jerusalem, and officers' clubs all over the country.

Like most people, we avoided going out at night during this period. We lost track of our friends from the Sword of the Spirit. Most of all, we missed the good times we had had with our dear friend, Father Curtin.

I saw Father Curtin one day while visiting the Holy Sepulchre Church. I spoke to him after the religious services. He told me that, like the other priests of his congregation, he went out occasionally during daylight, but never at night. They had received threatening phone calls from terrorist groups, telling them that they were enemy targets and should watch their step. He said that he had been harassed by some young thugs at dusk one day when returning to the convent from an errand. The boxing he studied as a young man had come in handy.

Finally, he informed me that he was being offered the position of assistant parish priest in a London working-class suburb. However, he had to solve a major problem first.

I avoided looking directly into his eyes. He said, "I don't mind telling you about it, Jacob. I actually came here today to pray for a miracle."

"Whatever it may be," I said, "I earnestly hope it will be granted."

He stared at me silently for a while. Then he said, "I very badly need a black suit. I don't have one. I cannot wear my frock in the streets of London. With all the rationing regulations and my meager income, I am desperate."

By this time we had left the church and were on our way home. I racked my brains in search of a way to alleviate the plight of this dear person. By the time we reached our house, a block from his convent, I had an answer. I insisted he come in. I almost dragged him, though I understood his reluctance and his fear that being late would engender anxiety in his community.

My wife was pleasantly surprised to see him. While they talked, I excused myself and left the room. I came back carrying an oversized black evening suit, and said, "Father Curtin, God has heard your prayer. I hope this will solve your problem." Then I handed him the suit.

He was speechless. His eyes seemed to pop out of their sockets. I continued: "As a Jew, my father-in-law could take no cash with him when he left Germany just before World War II. However, he could take any personal belongings as long as they looked used. He bought this suit as an investment and wore it once to make it look rumpled. When he arrived in Jerusalem, he gave it to me so I could have it tailored to my size, but I have no use for it. As you know, my father-in-law is an agnostic Jew. If you don't mind wearing a suit that was worn once by him, it's all yours. I can't think of a better use."

He took the suit and inspected it. He said, "Jacob, my bosom friend, not only do I not mind; on the contrary, I consider it Godsent. It is new and very large; it could easily be altered for me by our tailor. I have a suspicion that our late founding father, who was born a German Jew, has engineered this whole trick."

Then, turning to my wife, he said, "Stephanie, I am now ready for the glass of brandy you offered before. I'm shaking all over with excitement. God bless your family."

Jacob with the growing pigs in the backyard of the house in Jerusalem.

The Pig-Breeding Craze

Most of the pork products consumed in Palestine were imported, either from as far away as Holland or from Cyprus, which was a few hours distant by sailing ship. Most farmers in Palestine were either Moslems or Jews. The religion of both these peoples prohibits the eating of pork, so of course they did not breed pigs.

As the Mediterranean became a focus of battle during World War II, it also became the graveyard of many Allied ships carrying vital war material to the armed forces fighting in the Middle East. Holland and the other North Sea nations were occupied by Germany. The waters around Cyprus were infested with German and Italian submarines. Thus the meager quantity of pork products that reached Palestine was sold at premium prices.

The Christian rural minority around Bethlehem saw a chance of striking it rich by going into the pig-breeding business. Following the law of supply and demand, the few available pigs were sold at astronomical prices. When an epidemic wiped out a large number of these creatures, many families lost their life savings; others lost their homes and businesses, which they had sold in order to invest in pig-raising. There were tales of women who deprived their babies of milk, and instead breastfed piglets who had lost their mothers. Some people slept on the floor while they nursed sick pigs with loving care in their own beds.

We too were tempted to take part in this craze. Luckily, we gave up because of lack of space. We were also afraid our fanatic Jewish neighbors would unhesitatingly poison any pigs kept in the area.

After World War II ended, both the Jews and the Arabs of Palestine felt they had been double-crossed by the British Mandatory powers. They committed acts of terror against the government and its armed forces. To protect the administrative offices and their personnel, the authorities created military zones in Jerusalem surrounded by double walls of barbed wire, with access only through gates guarded by armed soldiers. Only people with special passes, issued by the security office, were allowed to enter.

A minority were permitted to keep living in their homes when these were absorbed by the military zones. The rest were forced to leave. Being Armenian, I managed to convince the security people that my family was neutral in the quarrel. We were issued zone passes and went on living in our house when our neighbors were sent away.

The large building next to our dwelling, which had been a seminary for young rabbinical students, became a billet for the sergeants of the British Military Police. They converted the first floor into a sergeants' mess and a bar. As their only civilian neighbors, we were welcome there. We were staggered by the amount of food wasted in their kitchen, and mentioned this fact to our aunt, Soeur Justine, who was now a nun in the convent of St. Joseph in Bethlehem. We said, "One could raise a few pigs with all that waste."

Two days after our visit to Bethlehem, while I was away at work, my wife Stephanie heard a knock and opened the front door of our house. Outside stood an armed soldier who said, "Excuse me, Lady, there is a nun outside looking for you." Stephanie stepped outside and was struck speechless. There was our aunt from Bethlehem, seated in the back seat of the convent's chauffeured black limousine, with three tiny marzipan-like, curly-tailed pink piglets at her feet, nestled in the folds of her ample black skirt.

Soeur Justine hadn't wasted any time after hearing our story of the leftover food. She had bought the three piglets for us at her first opportunity. When she was stopped at the gate on her way to our house with them, the goodhearted officer in charge found that she had no pass. Instead of turning her away, he sent the courteous young soldier to escort her to our house.

Thus began our experience with pig-raising. Luckily, we had inherited an empty storeroom behind our house from some people who were evacuated when the area became a military zone. This room sheltered the pigs during the night and in bad weather. When the weather was good, they spent the day outside in an enclosed yard. Thanks to the plentiful swill from the sergeants' mess, which we mixed with bran, these tiny creatures put on weight very rapidly.

We learned quite a bit about the behavior of pigs as ours grew up. Pigs are generally thought to be dirty animals that will gobble anything. In fact, our animals shunned dirty or spoiled food. They always relieved themselves in the same corner, and slept in a clean dry spot. They were very playful, even mischievous. They came running whenever they saw us, expecting to be talked to, petted, and rubbed behind the ears. Our children had lots of fun with them.

Of course, there were some episodes which may sound hilarious now, but were terribly unpleasant at the time. Once someone left the door open and the pigs wandered out of our backyard. They were brought back by the sentry of the zone gate, a few blocks away. Another time, when I was away for a week in Haifa on business, my wife and children came down with scarlet fever and Stephanie's mother had to take care of the pigs. They scared her to death. As she tried to feed them one day, a huge Arab who resembled a genie came toward her, adding to her terror. It was Jebrin, our fierce-looking but gentle Arab handyman, who stepped aside to let her run for her life. He had been hired to do the dirty work, and got busy right away with his chores, but Stephanie had a hard time convincing her mother that he was entirely harmless.

When the pigs were nine months old they were ready to be slaughtered. It was December and the security situation was getting worse, so there was an acute shortage of meat. We realized a good profit from what we sold.

From the meat we kept for ourselves, Stephanie chose a huge fresh ham to be roasted for a memorable Christmas dinner. We invited many friends and, of course, most of the sergeants from the Military Police. They attended the festivities in shifts. The ham was consumed together with large amounts of German potato salad — one of Stephanie's specialties — and washed down with beer or wine. Then we had coffee with whipped cream, homemade plum pudding, and Christmas cookies. For those of us who smoked, the sergeants supplied cigars and cigarettes.

So ended our involvement in the pig-breeding craze.

In the Winter and Spring of 1940 the infamous Fauzi el Kutub engineered numerous terrorist bombings including the destruction of the *Jerusalem Post* building (above) and Ben Yehuda Street (below).

The Blockade of Jerusalem

In September 1947 the United Nations voted for the partition of Palestine into the Jewish and Arab states. The Jews accepted the decision but the Arabs refused to go along with it. They said they had been in the country for over a thousand years and were not ready to give up their birthright to the land. They defied the United Nations resolution by attacking Jewish transportation on the highways and by sneak bombing of the Jewish quarters. One of their strategies was to force the surrender of the New City of Jerusalem by blocking the highway to Tel Aviv, the main supply source. Many battles were fought in Bab el Wad, the principal artery connecting Jerusalem with the Mediterranean. This highway turned into a graveyard of all kinds of supply vehicles rushed to Jerusalem to alleviate acute shortages of food in the New City. The visitor to the Holy Land, even now, can still see the skeletons of cars at the side of the road, surrounded by wreaths of flowers in memory of those who fell while helping the besieged people of the new quarters of the Holy City.

The Arabs also cut off food supplies to the New City from the old city. We lived in the New City and could get a limited supply of food from the old city. We were short of meat and fresh vegetables for a long time. I heard that everything was plentiful in Bethlehem, and went there once a week to buy pork and other supplies for my family and friends.

One day I boarded a service cab in Bethlehem. It already carried three other passengers: Father Khoren, an Armenian priest, sat in the front seat next to the driver and two Arab passengers were seated in the back. I placed my shopping basket full of supplies at the front, next to the priest's feet. I then took my place in the back with the two Arabs. The cab proceeded toward Jerusalem.

Before we reached the boundary of Jerusalem, we were signaled to stop by an armed Arab guard. As soon as I saw him, I said to the priest in Armenian, so the others could not understand, "Father Khoren, please cover my basket with your robe."

Turning around, he said, "Hagop, you dog son of a dog, is this one of your practical jokes?"

"No, Father, I swear this is serious. I'll explain later. Pretend not to speak Arabic."

The driver stopped the car and said, "I am cleared by the boycotting committee. They issued me a permit to drive on this road — here it is."

"Yes, I know you," said the guard, "but I was ordered to stop and search every car coming from Bethlehem. Don't be angry with me." He then called his helpers, who opened the doors and asked us to get out. The priest tried clumsily to get out with us, but the guard said, "No, not you, Father, you keep seated."

The back seat of the car and the trunk were searched thoroughly, but out of respect for the priest the front seat was not searched. Then the guard told the driver, "You can leave now."

The driver asked, "May I ask what you are looking for?"

The guard replied, "We received information from Bethlehem that somebody bought pork and other foodstuffs. He is on his way to Jerusalem to deliver them to the Jews. He has to come this way, so we'll catch him."

As we got under way, Father Khoren turned around, saying in Armenian, "Hagop, what has happened? You seem to know."

"Yes, Father," I replied, "I do know. They were looking for the basket covered by your robe."

He turned pale. "But why?" he asked.

I said, "The shortage of decent food in Jerusalem forces me to go to Bethlehem to get good pork and a variety of fresh produce for my family and friends. I do it once a week on my free afternoon from work."

"This is a dangerous game, Hagop," said the priest.

"Why?" I asked. "I'm not doing anything illegal."

"But who sent the guard?" he asked. "No car coming from Bethlehem is ever stopped."

I answered, "I usually buy pork from the same butcher — he treats me very well because I buy large quantities. But this time, when I went to his shop, he had what looked to me like the meat of a slaughtered sick animal. I told him I didn't like the look of his meat, and that unless he had something better I would have to look somewhere else. The butcher said, 'You can't do this to me. I especially killed this animal for you because I know that you come every week to buy from me.' I answered, 'I will buy the same quantity as usual from you, but not from this sickly-looking meat.' As I walked away, he called after me, 'Okay, smart guy, I'll fix you!' I went and bought the week's meat from another butcher. The disgruntled butcher must have phoned the Arab blockade committee to report that a blockade runner was on the way to Jerusalem with a quantity of meat for delivery to the Jews in the New City, and they sent the guards to check."

"Dear God!" exclaimed Father Khoren. "Please be careful. It could be dangerous. I will say a special prayer for your protection."

"You are very kind, Father," I answered. "I appreciate your concern and your prayer."

Jacob's daughter Gabriella with British soldier at the sandbag checkpoint.

Jacob's son George playing with British soldier's machine gun.

A Reign of Terror

In April 1948, my family — I, my wife, and my three children, aged eight, six, and two — were living in one of the three British Military Zones that the Mandatory Government had created in Jerusalem after World War II as a buffer between the Arab and Jewish quarters, which began fighting again after a lull during the World War II years. Each side claimed to be the rightful owner of Palestine. The British had promised, in the Balfour Declaration, to help the Jews to create a national homeland; at the same time, through Sir Henry McMahon, they had promised Palestine to the Arabs. Another reason for the creation of the British Military Zones was to protect the British armed forces from the constant bombing and shooting by Jewish terrorist gangs, of which Menachem Begin, the present Prime Minister of Israel, was a leader.

As a result of the constant unrest and bloodshed, a United Nations Commission of Inquiry recommended that the country be partitioned between the Arabs and the Jews, with a provision to create International Zones for the administration of the Holy Places in Jerusalem, Bethlehem, Nazareth, and Tiberias. The recommendation was approved by a vote in the General Assembly of the United Nations. The British government was asked to remain in Palestine to implement the partition decision, but irresponsibly refused to do so, and set the fifteenth day of May as the end of its mandate. At this time, the last British military and civilian personnel would leave the country without waiting for the formation of an authority to take over the administration of the country. The Jewish Agency promised to abide by the decision of the U.N. and began preparing an Israeli government to administer the Jewish half of the country, but the Arabs, under pressure from the neighboring Arab states, rejected the partition and vowed to fight any Jewish State. Instead, they created an independent Palestinian State with representation of only the minority Jews who had been in Palestine prior to the great Jewish immigrations of the 'thirties and 'forties, first when Jews fled to Palestine to escape Nazi persecution and, after the defeat of Germany, when the survivors of the concentration camps were freed and had nowhere else to go.

The result was a reign of terror. The Arabs blocked the highways connecting the New City of Jerusalem, where the Jews lived, from the rest of the land. They prevented food supplies from reaching the Jews in an attempt to starve them into surrender. They also blew up the pipelines bringing water to the Jews. The Jews retaliated by indiscriminately dumping fifty-five-gallon barrels full of explosives from armored cars into areas dense with Arab pedestrians, such as the Jaffa Gate and the Damascus Gate of the old city of Jerusalem, killing and maiming hundreds of people. Then the Arabs blew up the offices and press of the *Palestine Post*, the only daily English-language newspaper. One Sunday morning we were awakened by a loud explosion that shook the foundation of our house and showered us with broken glass from our windows. We later learned that this was the effect of a time bomb placed in a truck full of explosives parked in Ben Yehuda Street, a few blocks from our houses and from the center of the Jewish Quarter.

Bullets flew over our house as the Arabs fired on the Jews from the east side and the Jews answered from the west. I performed a dangerous task. Whenever there was a lull in the shooting, I had to get onto the roof to replace the tiles that had either been broken or blown away by the explosions all around us. Let me again mention that as we lived in the British Military Zone, we were safe as long as we remained in the area, but were exposed to as much danger as everyone else as soon as we left to go to work or shop or visit our relatives or friends. We also had the advantage of being able to move freely in both areas occupied by the belligerents. One guarded gate led us to the Jewish quarter and another to the Arab quarter. Since we were Armenian, and since I spoke both Hebrew and Arabic fluently, I was not molested by either side. I carried two identity cards. One, issued by the British authorities, said that I was Armenian. The other, issued to my wife by the Arab High Command, came in handy in areas under Arab rule.

Both sides intensified their terrorist activities as the fifteenth of May drew nearer. The Jews initiated a thorough terror campaign, which created panic in the Arab population. In the middle of the night, they blew up the Semiramis Hotel, which was situated in the fashionable Christian quarter of Katamon, where non-belligerent families had taken refuge after leaving their homes where they did not feel secure. Whole families were wiped out, among them a vice-consul of a European country. Our dentist, Dr. Sami Aboussouan, who was freed from the rubble by rescuers, was the only survivor from a large family.

The Arabs retaliated by blowing up the Jewish Agency, which was across the street from our backyard. The impact of the explosion cracked the walls of our house. Then the Jews wiped out the inhabitants of the whole village of Deir Yassim, which lay on the outskirts of the Jewish quarter.

The demoralizing effect of the bloodshed caused a full-scale exodus of the Arab population into neighboring countries, where they thought they would be safe. This was the origin of the Palestinian refugee problem, which remains unsolved to this day. Their homes, businesses, and other possessions were left behind and confiscated by the Israeli government as enemy property. The homes and businesses left behind by the Jews who fled the Arab quarter were looted by Arab ruffians and adventurers. While all this went on, the British Mandatory authorities shirked their duty of enforcing law and order. Instead, they acted like sulky children deprived of their toys. They kept their forces in the security zones and let all hell break loose around them.

Smoke billowing from the Jewish quarter on May 28, 1948, during the Battle of Jerusalem.

A Spy Suspect

When the United Nations General Assembly decided to partition Palestine we lived in a British military zone, which separated the Arab and Jewish sectors. Our home was across the street from the Jewish Agency, in the King George Avenue of Jerusalem. The Jews accepted the decision but the Arabs, who had lived in Palestine for over a thousand years maintained it was their country. However, they were ready to form a binational government with the Jews who had been in the country before the large influx of Jewish refugees fleeing Hitler's persecutions and the refugee camps. Many of these unfortunate people would have preferred to go to other countries, such as the U.S., Canada, and Australia, where they were not accepted. They had come to Palestine by necessity, not by choice.

Right after the Partition Decision, the Arabs began their sabotage. They attacked Jewish buses, mined the roads, and dynamited Jewish quarters and official buildings. The Jews retaliated by hurling drums full of explosives at Jaffa Gate and Damascus Gate, main entrances to the old city, killing and maiming hundreds of people.

The British, who had the Mandate over Palestine, seemed unable or unwilling to maintain law and order in the land. The United Nations asked the British to enforce the partition resolution. The British authorities replied that their security forces would leave Palestine on the eve of May 15, 1948, the effective date of the partition.

Our house was directly in the crossfire between the Arabs, aiming at the Jewish Agency, and the Jewish forces' retaliation. It finally got so bad that we left our house and took refuge in Bethlehem. No fighting was expected there, as the city was of no military value. In Bethlehem we lived in the convent of the Sisters of St. Joseph, a French religious order, where my aunt Soeur Justine was a nun. While my wife and children spent most of the time on the grounds of the convent, I met with other men, who like us had left their homes and had rented houses in Bethlehem and Beit Jala, a nearby village.

The fate of Jerusalem was the most common topic of our conversation when we met in cafés, where we passed our time drinking coffee, smoking water pipes ("Hubble-bubble"), and playing hand rummy.

One day I was seated in the Manger Square Café, engrossed in a card game, when I felt a tap on my shoulder. I turned and saw a sergeant of the Egyptian Armed Forces. Behind him stood a member of the Arab freedom fighters with his finger on the trigger of a machine gun. In a low voice, the sergeant said, "Please don't panic. Just get up quietly and follow me." I took his advice. When we reached the street, he pointed at the freedom fighter. "This gentleman claims that you were asking too many strategic questions about the fighting in Jerusalem. He accuses you of gathering information for the enemy."

I answered, "I know this man well. His name is Hassan. He was our butcher boy in Jerusalem. When he came to the café an hour ago, he said he had just arrived from there. I was one of many Jerusalemites who asked about the situation there."

The sergeant said, "I want you to walk with me, naturally, to the local police headquarters to investigate this accusation. Let us keep talking this way, as if we were old acquaintances, and avoid attracting attention. You know what happened last week to the nephew of the Mukhtar of Lifta." He was referring to the cruel incident in which a nephew of the Mukhtar (or selected elder) of Lifta, a village near the Jewish quarters of Jerusalem, had been torn apart in the marketplace by an unruly mob, to avenge his uncle's suspected collaboration with the enemy.

When we came to a crossroads, Hassan wanted us to go to the headquarters of the freedom fighters. The sergeant told him, "The Egyptian Regular Army is in charge of law and order. This investigation will have to be conducted by the official law enforcement authorities." Hassan did not like what he heard, and at this point he left. The sergeant said, "I cannot see how anyone can spy for the Jews. They are not to be trusted. Have you heard about the atrocities committed by them in Deir Yassin?" Deir Yassin was an isolated Arab village, surrounded by Jewish settlements. It was considered peaceful by the Jewish authorities. Its inhabitants kept to themselves and did not give trouble to their Jewish neighbors. At dawn of an April day in 1948, the unsuspecting sleeping villagers were attacked by two Jewish terrorist groups: the Irgun Zva'i Leumi (whose leader was Menachem Begin, who later became Prime Minister of Israel) and the Stern Gang, led by I. Shamir, who became Prime Minister of Israel after Begin. The terrorist groups were composed of young people of both sexes. After killing all the men, they raped the women and stole their valuables. They then subjected them to savage atrocities. They lined them up against a wall and sprayed them with machine gun bullets. They did not even spare the babies. They blew up the houses with dynamite. Only a few women survivors succeeded in getting away. Some children were wounded and hid under the corpses of their parents. (Reports by Jacques de Reynier, of the International Red Cross, and Richard C. Catling, Assistant Inspector General of the C.I.D. on April 13, 15 and 16, 1948, bearing the dossier # 179/110/17/GS, contain details of this massacre.) It was a calculated, diabolic strategy to create panic in Arab population centers. These centers were deserted at the slightest rumor of an impending Jewish attack.

When we reached the police headquarters, we met a young lieutenant of the Jordanian Army, a liaison officer to the Egyptian Army, who asked about my business there. When told that I was to be investigated for asking too many questions about Jerusalem, he raised his fist to hit me in the face and called me a pimp son of a bitch. The Egyptian sergeant stopped him, saying, "He is only a suspect. Let the police investigate this."

At the police station the duty officer wrote a police report stating the cause of my arrest, and giving my version of the events leading up to the arrest. I was then led to the Commandant's office. I was relieved when I recognized him, because he had a reputation for being fair. He asked me about my dealings with the Jews. I told him they were the same as everyone else. I had Jewish colleagues at work, Jewish neighbors, and some Jewish acquaintances, but since the trouble started, I had moved to Bethlehem and had no connection with any Jew.

He told me to undress in the next room, where I would be given a body check for signs identifying Jewish spies. A police officer checked all the parts of my body minutely, starting with the head: the ears, the nose, the inside of the mouth, the palate, the tongue, the gums; then the breasts, the armpits, between the fingers, my posterior, under my genitals, my legs, my feet and toes. He gave a satisfied smile when he reached my left little toe. "Stay as you are," he said, and he left the room. He came back followed by the station commandant. Pointing importantly to my toe, he said, "Here it is, sir! Here is the spy sign."

"What is the green color on your little toe?" the commandant asked me.

"This, Sir," I said solemnly, "is corn cure, which I bought from the Bethlehem pharmacy. It was specially prepared for me and they must have a record of it to confirm my statement."

"Okay," he said, and instructed the other police officer to get in touch with the pharmacy right away and report the result to him. Then he led me to his office and said, "I notice from your statement that you admit to possessing a gun."

"Yes," I said, "I carry a gun on the grounds of the St. Joseph's convent when I assist the regular night watchman." He asked whether I had a permit. I said I did not, because I never took the gun out. Several policemen were sent with me to the convent, where they searched our belongings and confiscated the gun — a 38-caliber Smith and Wesson, with all the ammunition I had.

Back at the police station, the bullets were examined by an expert who looked for flare bullets. I later learned these were used by spies to communicate with the Israelis. The ammunition expert reported that the bullets were ordinary ones.

While I waited for the result of the investigation, the assistant principal of the convent came to see the station commandant. She told him she had been sent by the principal with a message that the convent was under the protection of the French government, and if I was not released soon and my gun returned, she would ask the French consul to intervene.

The station commandant said, "There is no need for that. We find no reason to keep him any longer. However, you must understand that it is our duty to investigate every complaint." Then, to me: "I suggest you obtain a license from City Hall for the gun, which will be returned to you." We thanked him and left his office.

When I went to the desk of the duty officer to claim the gun, he said, "You must come tomorrow for it." Apparently he meant to keep it for himself. The Egyptian sergeant, who was still there, said angrily, "What do you mean, come tomorrow? Did you give him a receipt for it? Give him his gun right now!"

Upon reaching the convent, I was welcomed by the sisters. They wept with joy. The Mother Superior convened a Magnificat, or thanksgiving prayer service, in the convent's chapel. I could feel the genuine joy in the voices of the singers. It was good to be back.

Damascus, Pearl of the East

I was working at the Socony Vacuum Oil Company (Mobil Oil) in Jerusalem. A couple of days before the British moved out of Palestine, in May of 1948, Socony Vacuum decided to suspend its operations until the political situation cleared up. They paid us for May, and gave us an additional month's wages as a gesture of good will.

I joined my family in Bethlehem, where they had taken refuge because no fighting was expected there. We could hear the firing and explosions from afar. At night we could see the flames over Jerusalem. However, nothing happened in Bethlehem. I stayed there, unemployed, for a year. Then, when things quieted down, I was hired by the Christian Brothers in Jerusalem to teach English, French, math, and business courses, and to supervise the boarders in their dormitory.

In June of 1950, at the end of the school year, I received a letter from the Socony Vacuum Oil Company in Beirut, Lebanon. They offered me the job of helping to create a headquarters operation in Damascus for their business in Syria.

Syria and Lebanon were under a French Mandate for twenty years, from 1920 to 1941. Their combined finances were administered by a central treasury department, situated in Beirut. This arrangement, which continued even after both countries regained their independence from France, caused constant squabbling between the two countries. Husni el Za'im engineered the first Syrian military overthrow of the civilian government. He decreed that Syria should have its own independent financial administration, divorced from that of Lebanon. This was why Socony Vacuum, like other international companies doing business in Syria, was obliged to open main offices in Damascus to keep the local accounts ready for government inspection.

I readily accepted the job and reported to the main office in Beirut during the first week of July. I stayed up to the end of January 1951, when all the accounts of the company in Syria were computed as of January 1st of that year. With the new ledgers, I accompanied the other employees to Damascus.

Damascus is the oldest continuously inhabited city in history. Abraham passed through it on his way to the Promised Land. It is a welcome green oasis in the Syrian desert. When a traveler approaching from the East first sees it, he can easily think that it is a mirage and that his imagination is playing tricks on him. Damascus has been considered the Pearl of the East since antiquity. Haroun El Rasheed, who was made famous in the *Tales of a Thousand and One Nights*, neglected it in favor of his capital city of Baghdad. Baghdad has long since fallen into decay, while Damascus still lives in all its splendor. It has lush fruit and vegetable gardens, irrigated by cool, pure spring water from the snow-covered mountains. When the French occupied Damascus under the French Mandate, they called this crystal-clear water Vichy water, comparing it with that of the world-famous Vichy springs of France.

Before his conversion, St. Paul's supreme passion was the extermination of the Christians. The Christians were considered blasphemous heretics by the religious authorities of Jerusalem. On his way to Damascus on a mission to persecute the Christians, St. Paul fell from his horse and was blinded. His eyesight was restored by Ananias of Damascus, whom he had sworn to annihilate. St. Paul was transformed into a faithful preacher and ardent propagator of his new faith. He was lowered down to the outside of the city wall in a basket to escape his former allies, who wanted to to kill him for having defected to the Christians. Travelers can still visit a section of the ancient city wall, which is preserved as a historic relic.

Since I was not a Syrian citizen, when I went to Damascus the government issued me a temporary foreigner's work permit, to be replaced by a permanent one at a later date. I was separated from my family, who continued to live in Bethlehem because it was uncertain whether I would get a permanent permit in Syria.

I retain fond memories of the days I spent in Damascus. I passed many gratifying hours in the Souk, or Bazaar. It is completely covered by a large roof to provide protection from the burning desert heat of summer and the icy winds of winter. I explored its many workshops, fascinated by the skilled craftsmen who create brocades, carpets, leatherwork, inlaid woodwork, metalwork of gold and silver filigree, and Damascene blades of the famed Damask steel. I explored the historic sites, such as the tomb of Saladin, the imposing Great Mosque Jami Al Umawi. This tomb was built within the enclosing wall of the Temple of Adad in the First Century A.D. It was later replaced by a church dedicated to St. John the Baptist, built by the emperor Theodosius in the year 379. I partook of the most interesting and savory meals and the most delicious fruits in the local restaurants.

Damascus is located at the edge of the Arabian desert. On summer nights most of its people are outdoors, some in enclosed gardens which usually have a water fountain in the center. The males of the houses that have no garden congregate in front of their houses, conversing with their neighbors, while the women stay indoors and stew in their own sweat. The city water tankers spray the street with water to bring relief from the sweltering heat. One hears a "clip-clop, clip-clop" — the sound of the kibkab (a kind of shoe with a wooden sole, a high heel, and a leather strap). It is worn by the young boys and girls who carry empty pitchers to be filled with cool water from the fountain.

Squatting near the fountain are peasants whose baskets are piled high with romaine lettuce. They do a brisk trade, because almost every passerby buys at least one head of lettuce, washes it at the fountain, and eats the crisp vegetable while walking along.

A bit further on, a wailing Arabic music is heard, broken up by a "tick-tock, tick-tock" noise that comes from an open-air café. The café has a large circular pool in the center, in which goldfish swim. Tall jasmine bushes are covered with flowers which fill the surrounding air with their fragrance. Patrons seat themselves at tables all around the pool. Some play cards, others backgammon or dominoes. The "tick-tock" sound is caused by the backgammon players, who, after throwing the dice, slap the stones into the backgammon tray. All the games have some spectators, who supply noisy free advice for the players. Almost all the patrons smoke Hubble Bubble (the water pipe). A special coarse tobacco, called tombac, is smoked in the Hubble Bubble. It is soaked in water for a few minutes, then the water is squeezed out and a cake of the wet tombac is formed. This is placed on top of a hollow earthenware bowl, which is placed on a brass pipe immerged in water in a glass bottle. A piece of charcoal is placed on the wet tombac. The smoke which goes through the water is then sucked up through a flexible pipe. Hashish is sometimes mixed with the tombac. It is supposed to have a relaxing effect on the nervous system.

Sometimes special entertainments are offered by a troubador, a lyric poet, who sits on his haunches in the middle of an elevated canopy, playing a one-stringed violin called a roubabah. He relates his tale, stopping from time to time to play his wailing instrument to emphasize some point in the story.

This tale could be a hair-raising exploit from the life of the great Abu Zeid Bin Hilal, the brave warrior Antar Ibn El Abbas, or any other Moslem hero. There is a climax to every tale. It is awaited eagerly while a deep hush hovers over the spectators, who listen attentively. They rub their hands, their beards, or the undersides of their chins, not wanting to miss the smallest detail of the narration, now and then nodding approval.

Sometimes wrestling or belly dancing is performed on a portable stage. The performances last until midnight, when the heat relents and a cool breeze freshens the air.

My favorite pastime in Damascus was to visit the open air marketplace next to the old covered market ("Souk El Hamidy"). There I witnessed scenes that seemed to come from the *Tales of the Thousand and One Nights*. I heard merchants praising the qualities of the goods spread about them on the ground. I saw farmers with huge baskets full of freshly picked, delicious-looking, juicy fruit — apricots, plums, cherries, peaches, strawberries, mulberries, figs. They described the invigorating potency of their produce in melodious voices.

Next to the farmers, a tray of sweetmeats was perched on a rickety tripod. The owner urged people to buy his product (on which the flies were running races) in order to sweeten their family relations and win the good will of their mothers-in-law. A vendor of salted melon and pumpkin seeds coaxed the people to buy his wares to keep their jaws busy instead of sitting idle and falling asleep. A long line of customers waited to have their heads and beards shaved by a fierce-looking barber, who would seat them on a fragile crate in unsanitary surroundings.

Smoke drifted from an open-air kitchen, where a cook's helper was busy roasting pieces of meat strung on iron rods on top of an open charcoal brazier. Customers could eat their meat in a flat bread (pita) as a sandwich, or with rice, beans, and chick peas (garbanzo beans) in tomato sauce, served in earthenware pots. They sat on wooden benches or in any place they could find.

A lemonade vendor called upon the thirsty to quench their thirst with his rose attar mixed with cool water from the fountain of health (a famous fountain). In the livestock market, besides sheep, goats, donkeys, horses and camels, there were stacks of bags full of wheat, barley and animal feed from the fertile fields of Hauran (an extension of the Beka' Valley) as well as rugs of various patterns made of dyed sheep's and camel's wool by Bedouin women.

A large crowd surrounded a seller of medicine. I heard him say, "Come nearer, O faithful followers of our Lord Prophet Mohammed! The last and greatest messenger of the Almighty!" He extended his right hand, which held a bottle containing pink liquid, and continued, "I have a supply of the gift of health, in bottles like this one. An aged holy dervish was inspired to find this mixture, which is distilled from rare herbs.

"This holy man is at the end of his days — may he live to be a hundred and ten! He refuses to divulge the secret formula of the mixture! You may be the lucky people to buy the last batch. This liquid has the power to miraculously cure the ailments of body and soul. For your toothache, just rub a few drops on the gums around your tooth — within a few minutes the ache is gone, never to return! For stomachache, take five drops of this God-given wonder drug in a glass of water. It will dissolve your ache away. Head, ear, nose aches, and all other aches of the body and torments of the soul are likewise chased away by this wonder drug. Come forward, worthy citizens of this magnificent city of the Khaliphs and the great protector of Islam, Salah el Din el Ayubi (Saladin) of blessed memory, avail yourselves of this unique opportunity! When you seek me out to buy more, I shall be far away, for I am only passing through this holy city. I will be on my way after paying my respects and praying in the Holy Shrine of the Omiad Mosque." This mosque, formerly a church dedicated to St. John the Baptist, was built by the Emperor Theodosius I in 379 A.D.

At this point the speaker breaks the seal of the bottle he holds, sticks its neck into the mouth of the nearest spectator, then pulls it back harshly from the closed lips, saying, "Well, brother, what do you think?" Without waiting for an answer he continues, "My dear Moslem brothers, come forward! Have fifty piasters ready for each bottle. I recommend that you buy two or more bottles if you can." A pound is one hundred piasters and four pounds are equivalent to a United States dollar. A stampede of buyers ensues. Some pull out crumpled paper money from their pockets; others bring forth small coins worth two and a half, five, and ten piasters. They count the money into his extended left and snatch a bottle from his right.

By the time ten minutes have gone by, only a few bottles are left. Ater the rush is over, a thin voice comes from an old man in rugged clothes. He rubs his hands together and says, "Charitable Sir, I have only forty-five piasters. Would you sell me a bottle of the drug to relieve my aching limbs? May our great prophet reward you!"

The vendor replies, "All right, old father." He takes the old man's money, counts it before putting it in his pocket, and hands him a bottle of the rose-colored concoction.

I was warned by my Damascus friends to stay away from kids who play hide-and-seek and from men who are fighting. "They are very skillful pickpockets, and they have a field day in crowded places."

The Damascus merchants are a very shrewd lot. The story which follows illustrates their fame.

A merchant brought some goods to sell in Damascus. While waiting in an inn for the next day's market, he called to a child playing in the compound. The merchant gave the youngster twenty-five piasters (about six cents) to buy him some food that would fill him, feed his donkey, and help him to pass the time. After a short absence, the child came back carrying a watermelon and said, "Sir, I brought you this blessed juicy fruit. It will satisfy your hunger and thirst, the rind will feed your donkey, and the seeds will keep you busy."

At this the merchant said to himself, "How could I do business in this town? If the children are so smart, I dread facing the grown men!" The next day he went to another town to dispose of his wares.

Meanwhile, my work progressed satisfactorily under pleasant conditions. The Syrian authorities renewed my work permit for three months after my first month in Damascus. At the end of those three months, the manager telephoned me to say, "Jacob, the General Manager from Beirut would like to see you in my office." When I reported to the office, the General Manager said, "Sit down, Jacob." He pointed to a chair beside the desk. He then announced, "The Syrian authorities have discovered your wife is Jewish. They refuse to renew your work permit. I pleaded your case with them, but they would not change their decision." I had twenty-four hours to leave Syria.

On my last night in Damascus, I happened to mention to my landlady that I couldn't understand why so many of the local people had blond hair and blue eyes. She answered, "It's a pity you have to leave tomorrow. It's Family Picnic Day." I stared uncomprehendingly. She continued, "At the time of Saladin's rule, all the men were away fighting the enemy. When they did not return by springtime, the women got restless and were ready to riot. The governor of the city sensed trouble, so he sent a town crier to announce that the men would be returning the next day. The crier told the womenfolk to go to the outlying fruit orchards to welcome the men. In reality the men were far from coming back. At the same time, the prison authorities were instructed to tell the Crusaders, who had been captured in battle, that the next day was a holiday for them. The prisoners were taken to these same fruit orchards.

"You can imagine the result of this encounter between the eager women and the prisoners, who had long been starved for female companionship. Most of them had blond hair and blue eyes.

"The date of that encounter was proclaimed Family Picnic Day. It is celebrated every year by the womenfolk — they picnic in the outlying fruit orchards."

Omayed Mosque in Damascus, formerly the Cathedral of St. John

Legionnaire's Adventure in Indo-China's Jungle

While living in Damascus, Syria in 1951, I was introduced to a former legionnaire of the French Foreign Legion. He was a German married to a local woman. He had stayed behind when the French moved out, after their Mandate over Syria had expired. He related the following episode to me; it occurred while he was stationed in Indo-China, or Vietnam as we know it now.

We were once on patrol in Indo-China, hunting for Communists in the jungle. In the middle of the wilderness, we came across a pagoda, a Chinese temple. We got out of our car and surrounded the place. Our Commanding Officer led a detachment into the courtyard. They were stopped at the temple's entrance by two live tigers, who were leashed on either side of the door to protect this sacred place from desecration. The C.O. hesitated briefly, then ordered the machine-gunning of the beasts. At once he was addressed by a Buddhist monk, dressed in immaculate white garb, who appeared as if out of thin air.

In perfect French, the monk asked very softly what we were looking for and whether he could be of any service. Our C.O. told him we suspected there were Communists hiding in the temple, and wanted to search it.

The monk smiled, produced a small bamboo flute out of his pocket, and began to play a melancholy tune. At the sound of the flute, the two tigers retreated into their niches at the sides of the temple entrance. The way was now clear for us to enter.

After penetrating to the inner chamber, we saw a statue of Buddha in the center. Two rows of small elephants, made of solid gold, led to the statue. I counted fifteen on each side.

After our search we confiscated the elephants. Each of us hid his loot in the safest place on his body, and we went back to our car. I was the driver, so I hid my gold figurine in the tool box and locked it. We stopped at the next army canteen to get refreshments. When I came back to the car, I heard loud curses from the men who had preceded me. They were looking for their elephants and could find them nowhere.

I felt quite important. I thought I was the most cunning of the lot, having hidden my elephant in the locked tool box. You can imagine my consternation when I unlocked the tool box and found no elephant there. Our C.O. got really mad when he found that his elephants had also disappeared from the front seat, where he had left them.

We looked everywhere in vain. We were assured by the sentry that nobody had gone near our car while we were in the canteen.

The C.O. ordered us back to the pagoda. There we found the monk, still playing his flute in the yard. He greeted us with a graceful bow and a smile, in which we would later recollect a touch of mockery. We were too eager to enter the inner chamber to notice his attitude at the time.

We were bewildered by what we saw. I rubbed my eyes in disbelief when I saw all the elephants standing in their original places. It was as if they had never been moved.

While we stared in silence, our sergeant noticed a silken rope hanging from the ceiling. He reached for it and was immediately warned by the monk, who had followed us: "Don't pull the rope. It is dangerous."

The sergeant ignored the warning. As he touched the rope, he felt a sudden pain in his arm and let it go. He complained of a stiffness in his hand, and later in his whole arm.

We panicked and fled. We felt we were in a haunted place. Upon reaching the outer gate, our sergeant collapsed and lay inert on the ground. The C.O. became furious at this. He took out his revolver and aimed it at the monk, who had followed us. A large boa appeared — from God only knows where — and rushed at the C.O.

Our sergeant was dead. Carrying his body, we fled to our car and back to camp. A post-mortem examination showed nothing unusual. The doctor could tell us only that his death was due to a heart failure.

Apparently, said the legionnaire, the Buddhists have attained a higher degree of knowledge than our modern scientists.

Beirut, the Cultural and Business Capital

I reported to the general manager of the Socony Vacuum Oil Company the day after my arrival in Beirut. He said, "I am sorry I could not help you in Damascus. We do not have a job for you in Beirut. Even if we had an opening, you would have the same trouble as with the Syrian authorities. Please report to our cashier tomorrow. He will have a check for you covering severance pay. If I can help in any other way, feel free to call on me."

I told him, "As a matter of fact, I have a big favor to ask of you. I would like to work for the United Nations Palestine Refugee Agency. The headquarters are in the UNESCO building in Beirut. They are customers of your company. I would be very grateful for a personal recommendation." He phoned the company personnel manager, telling him, "Jacob is coming to see you in a few minutes. Arrange the proper contact for him in the United Nations. Give him all the help he needs." He told me, "I am sure that with your qualifications and experience you will have no problem landing a job at the United Nations. I wish you the best of luck."

By the time I arrived at the personnel manager's office, he had already contacted the personnel manager of the United Nations and had been told that they were very much interested in me. He told me to come back in the afternoon to pick up an application form for employment with the United Nations, which was being sent to him for me. That afternoon I filled out the application form and left it with the Socony Vacuum personnel manager, who promised to send it along with his recommendation.

Instead of waiting in Beirut for a reply from the United Nations, I went to Bethlehem to spend a week with my family. On my return to Beirut a letter and two urgent telegrams were waiting for me. The telegrams asked me to come to the personnel office of the United Nations at my earliest convenience for an interview. The next day I went to the UNESCO building and was interviewed by the accounting manager of the United Nations. He was impressed by my qualifications and experience. He offered me a job with a salary ten percent higher than I had been making at Socony Vacuum. I readily accepted. I was told that since the UNESCO building was in the suburbs outside Beirut, a special bus picked up the employees at designated stops and returned them after work. One could also pay for a seat in one of the very sharp-looking fleet of Model T Fords that plied this route. These cars were very popular in Beirut, and their drivers were proud of them and cared for them as showpieces.

I reported to work the next day. My boss was a middle-aged Swiss gentleman. The United Nations had inherited him from the International Red Cross when they took over the Palestine refugee relief work. He warmed up to me when I addressed him in German. He showed me their classification of accounts and asked me, "Do you think you could put this mess in order and write us a new manual?" I said, "I'll do my best."

He said, "You will have a stenotypist as your secretary. If you need more help just call the typing pool to send you what you need. I don't mean to rush you, but the quicker this mess is cleared up the more you will be appreciated."

I got to work right away.

I wrote to my wife that same day, gave her the good news, and asked her to join me with the children. We rented a furnished apartment, near the American University. It was a great relief for my wife and children to live again in a house with electricity and hot and cold running water, and to be able to buy whatever we needed from the overstocked shops. The transportation facilities were ideal. There were buses, streetcars and seats in passenger cars to take you anywhere along their route. After three years of primitive and confined life in Bethlehem, my family spent most of their time on the lovely white sand at the beach, and the children learned how to swim.

The Phoenicians lived in Lebanon in ancient times. The sea was their empire, and maritime trade the chief source of their fortunes. Timber of Lebanon was felled and provided an invaluable export. Phoenicia supplied lumber from the cedars of Lebanon and expert craftsmen to build King Solomon's temple in Jerusalem. Murex fisheries, chief source of a purple dye, were monopolies of the towns of Tyre and Sidon. Glass making and Phoenician handicrafts were other sources of income. King Hiram of Tyre and King Solomon of Judea (Israel) cooperated in business enterprises with North Africa. The Phoenician role was that of commercial intermediary between East and West. They were the first people to make extensive use of the alphabet, out of necessity for their business correspondence and bookkeeping.

Tyre, Sidon, Arward were powerful industrial and trading cities and separate independent kingdoms. They competed against each other, even helped foreign invaders to subdue their neighbors instead of forming a single strong political entity.

Nowadays Lebanon has two major population groups, the Moslems and the Christians. The Moslems are divided into three factions: Sunni, Druze, and Shia. The Sunni live mainly in the city of Beirut. The Druze is a dissident and secretive sect which split from the Shi'ite Moslems. The founder of the sect was a tailor in Persia (Iran). The name derives from *terzi*, meaning tailor in Persian. The Druze fled to Mount Lebanon in the eleventh century, after their leader, the Fatimite Caliph Hakim, was assassinated in Cairo, Egypt. Only about ten percent of their faithful, called the "Uqqal," or "Wise Ones," are allowed to read the full scriptures of their religion. They believe in reincarnation, and at the end only the chosen few among them will enjoy eternal life hereafter. They are fierce and unyielding warriors.

The Shia Moslems split from the mainstream Sunni branch of Islam soon after the death of Mohammed in 632 A.D., resulting from a political disagreement as to who should succeed Mohammed as Caliph, or leader of Islam. They make up the majority of the Moslems in Lebanon (and Iran). They are generally poor and not well educated. They presently form the Amal militia (*amal* means "hope" in Arabic).

The Maronites ("Al Mawarineh") form the most numerous Christian religious community of Lebanon. Their religion was instituted in the early Christian era by some monks who took refuge at Mount Lebanon from Hama in Syria, where they were persecuted by the Greek Orthodox on account of differences in their religious beliefs. Their language is Arabic. They conduct their liturgy (religious services) in West Syriac, which is similar to Aramaic, the language of Palestine after the captivity, and that spoken by Christ and his disciples. They are Roman Catholics, but their priests are permitted to marry, only once before they are ordained. A joke states, "In his first prayer of the day the religious Jew thanks God for having created him a man, not a woman, whereas a Maronite priest implores God to preserve his wife."

The Maronites' political power is centered on the Phalange Party of President Amin Gemayel. It was created by his father, Pierre Gemayel, after a visit to Spain in the 'thirties, where he was impressed by General Franco's Phalangists. The Gemayel family was involved in feuds with other Maronite clans ruled by two former Presidents, Camille Chamoun and Souleiman Franjieh. The two latter were also warlords with private militias.

The other Christian communities are the Armenians who came to Lebanon when they fled from the Turkish genocide before and during World War I. They prospered and acquired political clout. The remaining Christians include Greek Orthodox, Syriacs, Chaldeans, and other small minorities.

Some Jews also live in Lebanon. They have their own clubs, the Alliance Israelite Francaise. They were prominent before the Lebanese Civil War, but they now keep a low profile.

When Lebanon won its independence from France, an unwritten agreement required the President to be a Maronite Christian, the Prime Minister a Sunni Moslem, and the Speaker of Parliament a Shi'ite Moslem. The Moslems now want a greater representation in the executive and legislative branches.

Beirut is the capital of Lebanon and its chief port. According to legend it was here that St. George slew the dragon. The city was very much neglected under the Ottoman, or Turkish, rule. The French, who had the Mandate over Lebanon and Syria after World War I, revived Beirut. They did a very good job. It became one of the most important cosmopolitan cities in the Middle East. It had very good hotels, casinos, night clubs, and other entertainments to satisfy the most sophisticated visitor. One could swim and water-ski in the Mediterranean Sea in the morning, and enjoy skiing on the snow-covered mountains the same afternoon. Gourmet restaurants served the most exquisite European and Middle Eastern dishes. Beirut deserved the name, "Little Paris," given it by world travelers.

Business was booming, and if you had money you could buy anything made anywhere in the world. Beirut had one of the most important gold markets, and a bonded custom-free warehouse of goods from all over the world, ready to be shipped anywhere. It had the American University, the Jesuit University, and the National University, besides some smaller ones. Students from all over the Middle East, and some from Europe and the United States, were eager to enroll in the Beirut universities. Their standards of education were high.

We often had lunch in a restaurant that jutted out into the sea, and watched the fishermen catching fish with their nets. We were also fascinated to watch the different schools of fish following their leaders. Time passed very quickly on these occasions.

We took one-day trips to visit interesting places. Once we went to Byblos. To get there, we had to pass the Dog River ("Nahr el Kalb"), where we saw the inscriptions on the rocks in hieroglyphics, cuneiform, Greek, Latin, Arabic, English and French, in memory of the invading armies that had crossed the river, from Rameses II of Egypt and Nebuchadnezzar to General Allenby in World War I. The most recent inscription was by the combined British and Free French forces who ousted the Vichy French from Lebanon and Syria during World War II.

Byblos was chief center of the cult of Astarte and Adonis on the Phoenician coast. Adonis was killed by a wild boar while hunting. The Adonis river's annual red floods, resulting from iron deposits, symbolize the wounded god's blood. Afga is the source of the Adonis river and is the place where the god met his death.

The famous Ahiram's Sarcophagus has an inscription in a very early script, the ancestor of our alphabet. It was found in Byblos. Byblos was the chief harbor for the export of cedar and other wood to Egypt. The early Greeks received their papyrus through Byblos. The word "bible" comes from Byblos, i.e., "the papyrus book." Ruins of temples, remains of excavations, and Jebeil, a small Moslem town, are all that can be seen of Byblos at present.

We also visited the famous Cedars of Lebanon ("El Arz"). We saw the eternal snow on the mountain top. We were disappointed at seeing only two aging remnants of the cedars, a few hundred younger trees in all. Goats were running free, cropping the young shoots. Nothing was being done to create a National Park for a real forest. On our way back we stopped at the house where Khalil Gibran, known as the "Immortal Prophet of Lebanon," was born. At the foot of the mountain we visited an undergound cavern, with variously shaped stalactites and a café on an underground lake.

A few days before taking the trip to the Cedars of Lebanon, our youngest son, Johnny, who was six months old, had to be rushed to the American University Hospital clinic. My wife Steffi had noticed blood in his stool. The doctor said he had dysentery, prescribed antibiotics, and kept him in the hospital. He was to be under twenty-four-hour watch and expert treatment. Johnny must have been infected by the milk he was getting in Bethlehem. We were lucky that he was in Beirut where he could get the best medical care. When we first went to visit Johnny in the hospital, we were told not to take him out of his bed. On our second visit, he turned his face away from us when we talked to him. The nurse who was in the room noticed this behavior and told us, "Your baby longs to be picked up. He is very friendly when I pick him up." Steffi picked him up; he let out a deep breath and was all smiles.

In a way, Johnny being in the hospital made it possible for us to go to the Cedars of Lebanon. We could not have made it if we had him with us. The trip took many hours of bus riding and would have been too strenuous for him. We often took him with us to Antelias, the seat of the Catholicos Archbishop of Silicia of the Armenian Gregorian rite, who has a seminary for preparing the clergy. We spent many pleasant afternoons in cafés with swimming pools or waterfalls in the area.

On another occasion we visited the Beka' valley. It was one of the fertile valleys, important for its contribution to the granaries of the Roman Empire. The Turks of the Ottoman Empire neglected it and it turned into a desert. It is now being reclaimed and has already recovered part of its original fertility. Baalbek ("Baal of Beka' ") is an ancient religious site. The ruins of the Temples of Baalbek ("Lord of Beka' "), legacy of the Roman rule of the second and third centuries A.D., are to be seen there. Baalbek was the Greco-Roman town of Heliopolis.

After leaving Baalbek we stopped at an idyllic outdoor café at Zahleh, where we had a delicious Lebanese lunch and drank locally distilled Arak (anise brandy) at a table next to a brook. Zahleh is a Christian village, famous for its fruit orchards and for the Zahleh Arak, distilled from the fermented juice of the grapes grown in its vineyards.

In the meantime, my work was proceeding satisfactorily at the United Nations. The classification of accounts was basically sound. They must have been screwed up by a person who did not understand the system. It took me much less time than I had feared it would to straighten things up, with little overtime. I must admit that I had excellent help. My boss was elated when I surprised him one day with the completed work. He took a few minutes to go through the pages, stood up, and shook my hand. "I am speechless, my friend," he said. "Congratulations. I knew you could do it." We went to the typing pool together, and my boss asked the supervisor to have fifteen copies made right away, top priority, and fifty more copies to be ready for distribution to branch offices.

There was an executive meeting the next day. It included an English general, a French colonel, a Belgian colonel and some civilians representing their countries in the U.N. Each had a copy of my completed work in front of him. My boss proudly introduced me as the author. Back in the office, he gave me a letter informing me of a ten percent raise in my wages as of the day before. I was also appointed the highest authority on the matter of classification of accounts. After that date all problems, clarifications, and approvals had to bear my initials. I now settled down to an easy life and took short trips to the surrounding mountains, such as Aley and Bhamdoom, and Suk el Gharb, with my family to get away from the summer heat of Beirut.

I also had a clear head to do some thinking about the future. I began to look at life all around me with a clearer vision. I noticed that once you left "El Burje," the center of town, you were in a totally different world as you entered the residential quarters.

I had an uneasy feeling every time I passed through this area on my way to work — I was shocked at the poverty and the unsanitary conditions under which the Moslem population of this area lived. Except for a few rich families, the life of the Christian population, both in East Beirut and the Christian villages, was very simple, but comfortable. Their standard was far below what one might expect given the glamour and wealth of the business center and the glitter of the areas where the tourists congregate.

Public security was almost nonexistent. Housebreaking, assault, murder and other crimes were hardly ever solved. The police force, with sharp uniforms and high boots, looked like guards out of a comic opera. They seemed to be more for show than for public protection.

What I dreaded happened on July 13, 1951. I was on my way to El Burje, in a streetcar at 3 P.M., when I noticed a large number of cars speeding around us, going in the opposite direction. I heard the conductor remark loudly, "I wonder what happened downtown to scare all these people away!" He meant it as a joke. The nearer we came to downtown, the less traffic we saw going in our direction. When we got to the El Burje area, we saw what looked like the entire police force milling around. I asked a policeman why there were so many police there. He told me, "My advice for you is to ask no questions. Go home as fast as you can."

I took the next tram and headed back. We learned that evening on the radio that Riad el Solh, former Summi Prime Minster of Lebanon, had been shot in Amman, Jordan. Out of frustration, his followers attacked some businesses in downtown Beirut. The next morning we learned that some

Moslem gangs had gone on a rampage in the Christian quarter, killing people and looting houses. One week later, on July 20, 1951, King Abdullah of Jordan was killed in the Mosque of "Al Aqsa" in Jerusalem. The Moslems again tried to attack the Christians, but the Lebanese Army rushed its tanks to town and prevented the situation from getting out of hand. That night, I thought to myself, "We must leave this country before all the glitter fades away. When the white shining snow melts, it exposes all the ordure that it covered."

There were too many problems in Lebanon, mostly caused by the myopic behavior of its rulers. They were despots imposing a feudal system on the common people. They had forgotten the fable of La Fontaine, about the lion and the mouse, which they must have learned in their French classes at school. It reads as follows: The lion was dozing in the forest after a heavy meal, when he was disturbed by a mouse. He covered the mouse with his paw. The mouse pleaded for his life, saying, "O great Lord, have mercy on me and spare my life. I may be useful to you some day." This tickled the lion's sense of humor, and as he was in one of his rare good moods, he released the mouse with the following admonition: "You rascal, I will let you go this time, but I hold you to your promise." He knew in his heart that he would never see the mouse again. A few weeks later, the mouse heard the angry roars of the lion, blasting through the forest. Following the sound, he found him entangled in a hunter's net. He got busy gnawing at the net and freed the lion. The lion could not believe what had happened, but he learned a lesson for life. The leaders were too busy making money and spending it wastefully to realize that every citizen is vital to the wellbeing of the nation and is entitled to a decent living, the same as every cog in a wheel has to be well-oiled to keep a machine functioning properly.

The morning after the second riots I expressed my feelings to Steffi. She was not very happy about leaving the pleasant life of Beirut. She tried to persuade me that the Moslem riots were spontaneous expressions of a temporary frustration. Having lived under similar conditions in Palestine in the late 'twenties and early 'thirties, and then again in the 'forties, I had a presentiment that these were the first sparks of an all-consuming conflagration. I insisted on leaving.

We decided to go to Brazil, the only country that was booming at that time, to which we could get immigration visas without delay. We would have preferred to go to the U.S., but there was a waiting period of many years for visas. Thus, Steffi left for Bethlehem with Johnny, to liquidate what we still had there. During her absence, our other three children, George, Gabriella and Joseph, stayed in a vacation home run by nuns in the mountains.

My boss was quite disappointed upon hearing of my plan. He tried to sway me by offering me more money. He spoke of the dangers of taking a large family with little money to a country where I did not know the language or the customs, and had no job waiting for me. He even said, "Jacob, I will help you get a transfer to the United Nations General Headquarters in Lake Success, New York." Of course he gave no guarantee, and finally said, "I admire your courage. I am confident that with your perseverance you will succeed, even in Brazil."

After we got our visas for Brazil, we were told that the United Nations Refugee organization would pay for our sea passage, plus five dollars per day per person for the duration of the trip, since we were refugees. My mother and brother Levon came to Beirut to spend a few days with us and to wish us Godspeed. A cousin of my mother had a Persian rug store in Beirut. He advised us to invest some of our money in Persian rugs, and to sell them at a profit in Brazil. It proved to be a very good investment.

While walking in downtown Beirut a few days before we left, I met an Armenian friend whom I had not seen for years. He told me he had just returned from Brazil. He said if I went to the American Chamber of Commerce in São Paulo, Brazil, which was our destination, I could get a job in one of the American industries through that office.

We had only $350 cash with us, a few Persian rugs and a few gold coins. We were two grownups and four children, the oldest eleven years old and the youngest six days short of eleven months old. We sailed on the night of November 1, 1951, aboard the Greek ship S/S Corinthia, into the unknown.

The obelisks at the Temple of Byblos.

Jacob and his family soon after arriving in Brazil.

The Church of St. Sophia, built in the Fifth Century.

A Mission to Turkey

Early one Monday morning — it was September 27, 1977 — I was luxuriating in bed just after waking up, meditating while listening to the chirping of birds on a tree outside our second-story bedroom. It was a new experience for me. I had just retired from a job in the U.S. Postal Service, which had required me to rise at five every morning. I appreciated the comfort of this new phase of my life. No longer did I have to leap out of bed the moment I awakened, hurry into my clothes and hit the road without stopping for breakfast. As I thought of those winter mornings in which I had to get up in the dark, run outside, start my car, shovel the snow from the driveway, and rush to work, it felt doubly good to be in bed.

My daydreams were suddenly interrupted by my wife Stephanie. She was calling from the first floor to tell me my youngest brother, Archak, was on the phone, calling us from Amman, Jordan. Unless there was a special reason, we usually called each other only at Christmas and Easter.

Archak apologized for getting me out of bed, then inquired about us and our children. When the amenities were over, he said, "Sit down, Hagop. I want to discuss a matter of importance with you."

He told me that the previous day, while listening to an Armenian radio broadcast from Cyprus, he had heard that Kevork (George), the oldest son of our brother Dikran (Dick), was arrested in Turkey on charges of terrorist activities. "Hagop," he said, "we've thought the situation over. We discussed it with our brothers and sisters, our close friends, and our lawyers. We all believe that in view of your experience in handling people and your natural gift of communication — as well as your American citizenship — you would be the ideal person to go and save George. His mother Archaluz will have to go with you, to influence some hard-line Turkish prosecutor. Please discuss the matter with your family and find out how long it will take you to get a visa for Turkey, and let me know if you are ready to go. One thing more," he added, "don't worry about the expense. I'm ready to foot the bill."

Stephanie nodded her approval as I said, "I'll call our travel agent as soon as I hang up. I'll inquire about the visa and other travel information, and call you back in two hours."

I called the travel agent immediately. He told me American citizens didn't need visas for Turkey. TWA had direct flights to Rome from O'Hare Airport in Chicago twice a week, and Alitalia had daily flights from Rome to Istanbul. There would be no problem. I called my brother back, and we decided to meet in Rome within three days to work out a plan of action.

Now for some background about my nephew George. Our brother Dick was working as a purchaser at the U.S. airbase in Libya. When Muammar Kadafi asked the U.S. armed forces to leave Libya, Dick stayed on because he had property there which he couldn't dispose of on short notice. Kadafi ordered all Western schools closed and confiscated their property. Italy was welcoming refugees from Libya, which had been an Italian colony before World War II. Dick's wife Archaluz and their three children, George, Zaven and Sonia, moved to Rome for the school year and the children continued their education.

They spent their summer holidays with their father in Tripoli, Libya. George was a boarder at the Mekhitarist Armenian Catholic Fathers' College of St. Raphael Island in Venice. George later became a successful traveling salesman, representing well-known Italian shoe factories.

At the time of my brother's call to me, George had recently broken up with his girl friend in Rome and in Vienna he met an Armenian girl student from Istanbul. She invited him to her parents' home in Turkey. It was the time when Iran, under the Shah's rule, was buying everything that was offered, and every factory representative rushed to Teheran to get his piece of the pie. George could not resist this temptation, so he too decided to try his luck in Iran, but instead of flying there directly, he took the overland route, passing through Yugoslavia, Greece, and Turkey, to stop and visit with his new girl friend and her family.

When George applied for a visa to travel through Turkey, the staff at the consulate told him they knew about his anti-Turkish activities. George was the president of an Armenian youth club, and was involved in peaceful demonstrations. He made anti-Turkish speeches, and carried placards with derogatory slogans in demonstrations across the street from the Turkish Embassy in Rome. The consular officials told George that despite his political activities, he would not be barred from Turkey, which was a democracy and welcomed everyone. They issued him a travel visa.

George left in his Alfa Romeo a few days later. Not long afterward, the Turkish authorities detained him in Istanbul for subversive activities. That was the last news about him.

Three days after my phone conversation with my brother Archak, I arrived at the airport in Rome. He met me there, along with Archaluz and her son Zaven. They drove me to our brother Dikran's apartment. We all gossiped and exchanged the latest news about our respective families. Then we addressed the subject that brought us to Rome.

Archak said, "None of us has ever been in Turkey. I suggest we first visit the Armenian Catholic bishop in Rome and ask him for guidance." The Armenian clergy traditionally act as counselors to their people in civil matters.

The bishop himself was unavailable, and his assistant, who had family in Turkey, didn't want to get involved. He had heard about George's bad luck, and he tried to discourage us from going. "You don't know the Turks," he said, "they'll arrest you too."

Archak said, "All we want is a lead so we can hire a good lawyer to help us in Istanbul."

The clergyman replied, "You'll only bring trouble to the Armenians of Turkey."

Archak asked him what had become of the parable of the Good Shepherd, "who, when he lost one sheep, left the entire flock to search for the missing sheep." I remarked, "Jesus was speaking Aramaic, which our learned good friend, the assistant bishop, does not understand."

It happened that an Armenian priest of the Gregorian church was visiting the assistant bishop. This priest came to our rescue, telling us to go to the Armenian Gregorian Patriarch (Archbishop) in Istanbul, who would be happy to give us all the help we needed.

Suddenly the assistant bishop's attitude changed. He became very friendly, saying, "After all, you are Armenian Catholics. Go to our Archbishop in Istanbul and he will help you." He gave us the Archbishop's address, recommended a good hotel and restaurant, wished us good luck and gave us his blessing.

We returned to Dick's apartment and resolved to contact the heads of both the Armenian Catholic and Armenian Gregorian churches when we reached Istanbul. Archak had spoken with the Armenian Gregorian Patriarch of Jerusalem, who had recommended the Park Hotel in Istanbul because the owner was Armenian and a personal friend of his; we decided to stay there.

Archaluz and I took the Alitalia flight to Istanbul the next day. We went through the passport and customs formalities without a hitch. The cab we found looked as if it were held together with spittle and chewing gum. We heaved a sigh of relief when it deposited us at the hotel without any mishaps.

At the check-in counter of the hotel, we were told there was no vacancy. I asked to speak with the manager, and told him we came recommended by the Armenian Patriarch of Jerusalem, who sent his greetings to the owner of the hotel. The manager invited me to have a drink at the bar in the garden while he arranged some accommodations for us. We were given a suite with two bedrooms, a sitting room, and a balcony with a view of the Bosphorus and the upper city of Istanbul.

We called on the Armenian Catholic Archbishop after an early breakfast. We knew that the best time to find him was right after mass, before he got involved in his busy schedule. I told his secretary I was an Armenian Catholic from America and wanted to see his Eminence. The secretary replied that he was in his quarters, led us to the salon, and asked us to wait while he announced our visit.

After a short wait, the Archbishop appeared, wearing his purple fringed robe, a large gold cross hanging on his neck. He opened his arms to us, saying, "Welcome to our modest abode." We knelt on one knee according to custom and kissed the ring on his right hand, which Archbishops wear as Princes of the Church. He immediately raised us from our knees, saying, "Oh, please! Please!" Then he continued, "I understand you came from America. What part of the States are you from?"

I replied, "I live in Zion, Illinois, forty miles north of Chicago. This is my sister Archaluz. She lives in Rome." We related the events that brought us to Istanbul and asked his help in finding a lawyer to free George. He said he would discuss the matter with Father Anton, his legal assistant, who was a Mekhitarist priest. Mekhitarists are Armenian clergy dedicated to the education of Armenian youth. They have colleges in Venice, Vienna, Paris and other parts of the world. Father Anton is principal of the Mekhitarist college in Istanbul. He was a captain in the Turkish Army and knows all the important people.

His Eminence asked us to call on him in two days, at which time he was confident we would be put on the right track. In the meantime, he would pray and ask guidance for our cause and he recommended we do the same.

After we left the Armenian Catholic Archbishop, we took a cab to the Armenian Gregorian Patriarchate, which is in a suburb of Istanbul. The Patriarch is a venerable old man. He served as a priest in Jerusalem when he was newly ordained. As

Patriarch of Istanbul he travels a lot, and has been in most world capitals, including the Soviet Union, so he is quite well informed. He listened to our story, then spoke of it to his legal secretary, who informed him that it was being followed up since it concerned a young Armenian. However, so far the whereabouts of George had eluded him.

We told the Patriarch we had been advised to hire a Jewish lawyer, who could be more sympathetic to Armenians. Without commenting on our remark, he gave us the address of a famous Jewish lawyer. At the end of our visit he said, "I'm very happy that you came to see me. I know you belong to the Armenian Catholic Church, but I consider all Armenians to be my flock irrespective of their church affiliation. My door is open to all, and my resources are at your disposal. Please keep me posted on developments in your case and do not hesitate to call on me for help. Good luck and God bless you."

After lunch we went to see the Jewish lawyer. He said that he specialized in business matters. However, his young Turkish partner was a criminal lawyer, so he suggested we call in two days and talk to him. We gave him a general idea of the case and left.

On the way to the hotel, I suggested to Archaluz that we take sightseeing tours of the city to keep us busy, and see something of Istanbul as long as we were there. She welcomed my suggestion, so we booked seats on the tour entitled "Istanbul in One Day — Two Continents." At nine the next morning, we were driven to the old city over the Golden Horn through the Ataturk Bridge. We saw the Hippodrome, originally created by Septimus Severius in 203 A.D., inspired by the Circus Maximus of Rome. Two obelisks are prominently displayed in this area. The Obelisk of Theodosius I is one of the obelisks erected in the Temple of Karnak in 1471 B.C. by Tutmoses II of the 17th Dynasty. It was moved to Istanbul under the reign of Theodosius I in 390 A.D.

The second obelisk, of Constantine Porphyrogenitus, was covered with shining bronze plates. When the Crusaders invaded and mercilessly burned and sacked Constantinople (as Istanbul was then called) in the year 1204, they mistook the shining bronze for gold, so they vandalized the obelisk.

Next to the Hippodrome is the Blue Mosque (Sultan Ahmet). It is said that Sultan Ahmet's ego was hurt every time he saw the Christian Ste. Sophia Church and he decided to build a mosque that would surpass it by far in splendor. In his zeal to have it completed quickly, he worked every Friday on the site, helping the builders. The Moslem mullahs (religious leaders) resented the construction of six minarets on the mosque, because this equaled the number of minarets at the sacred Mosque of Kaaba in Mecca. Thus the Sultan was obliged to erect a seventh minaret on the Mosque of Mecca.

The architect Sedefkar Mehmet Aga, a student of the famous Koca Sinan (born a Christian but converted to Islam) was the builder of the Blue Mosque. This magnificent structure of huge proportions owes its name to the predominantly blue color of its interior. All the walls are covered with blue and green tiles and the 260 windows with stained glass. The Mihrab and Minber are of splendidly sculptured white marble from Marmara.

A short distance from the Blue Mosque is Ste. Sophia Church, which is now a museum. In 325 A.D. Constantine built the first basilica and named it Aya Sophia ("Divine Wisdom"). It was destroyed and restored a couple of times. The present grand structure was built by Justinian and all the parts of the Empire contributed lavishly for the erection of the holy structure. Columns of red porphyry, formerly given to the Temple of the Sun at Heliopolis, pagan monuments of Athens, Rome, Delphi and Baalbek were plundered. White marble from Proconnessa and clear green stone from the isle of Euboa — these are just a few items worth mentioning. In addition, all the resources of the Empire were devoted to purchasing gold, silver, precious stones and ivory for the magnificence of this holy place.

A solemn inauguration took place on December 27, 537 A.D. The Patriarch Menas welcomed Justinian, accompanied by the state dignitaries. At this occasion Justinian was so overwhelmed by the awe-inspiring splendor of the church that he cried, "O Solomon, I have bested you!"

After the conquest of Constantinople, on May 29, 1453, the Sultan Mehmet II ordered that the Ste. Sophia Church be converted into a mosque, and prayed in it on June 1. All the mosaics were preserved. Ataturk transformed the church into a museum.

One of the columns of Ste. Sophia has a hole in it, big enough to fit a finger into. It is always moist, due to osmosis, as its foundations are surrounded by water. It is claimed that this moisture has a healing power. People insert their fingers in the hole and rub the moisture on aching parts of their bodies to get relief. Barren women rub the moisture on their navels so they can conceive.

Our sightseeing guide was a Turkish Armenian. He showed me a mosaic depicting Emperor Basil II from an Armenian

Dynasty, Byzantine Emperor from 976 to 1025. Basil's reign marked the highest power of the Eastern Roman empire since Justinian I. The Comnenos Byzantine Dynasty (1081–1204) was of Armenian origin. Another interesting mosaic is that of the Empress Zoe of the Macedonian Dynasty. She was married several times. The mosaic shows her on the left hand of Christ, holding the Holy Bible. On Christ's right side is her second husband, Constantine Monomacos. The head and name of the Emperor were changed every time the Empress had a new husband.

The Czar Vladimir of Russia was unhappy that his nation did not belong to one of the great religions of his time. He ordered a commission to study the Moslem, Jewish and Christian religions. The Moslem and Jewish religions were not found to be convenient. When the emissaries who were sent to Rome and Constantinople returned, they reported that the services they attended in St. Peter's Church of Rome were impressive, but they were nothing by comparison with those performed in the Church of Ste. Sophia, where they felt themselves to be surrounded by a heavenly atmosphere. This experience prompted the Czar to choose the Greek Orthodox religion.

Vladimir received baptism in 989 A.D. and married a Princess of the Byzantine Imperial Family. He requested that missionaries be sent from Byzantium to Russia to convert the Russian nation to Christianity.

Ivan the Great of Russia married Sophia Paleslogus, niece of the last Byzantine Emperor. He adopted the Byzantine double-headed eagle (one looking east. the other looking west) as royal emblem and took the title "Tsar" or Caesar. This was done to present himself as heir of the Byzantine Empire.

The Catholic Church of Rome was infuriated by its failure to win over the Russians. This revived the devouring flame of Western hatred of the East. Rome finally succeeded in getting even with its rival when the Fourth Crusade overthrew the Byzantine Empire with the tacit connivance of the Papacy. The hostility between the West and the East is still alive and thriving in modern times.

A contributing factor to the success and popularity of the Eastern Church was that it encouraged the nations it converted to translate the Scriptures and celebrate the religious services in their own languages, whereas Rome imposed the Latin tongue on its converted peoples. Where no alphabet existed the Byzantines helped create one. Ulfila did this at the end of the

Fourth Century for the Goths. Sahak and Mesrob translated the Bible from Greek into Armenian, and in the Sixth Century the Gospel was translated into Hunnish for the Huns of the Caspian. Cyril and Methodius created an alphabet for the Slavs and translated the Holy Scriptures into their languages in the Ninth Century. These are a few of many deeds that endeared the Eastern Orthodox Church to the nations it acquainted with the Christian faith.

After Ste. Sophia, we were driven to the Topkapi Palace (the Old Seraglio). We saw the immense treasure accumulated by the Sultans over the years. The most impressive were the items in the Hall of Relics, where some hairs from the beard of the Prophet Mohammed are displayed in a glass enclosure. The coat and sword of the Prophet, as well as relics of other saints of the Moslem religion, are guarded in a locked sanctuary with a glass door.

One member of our tour was a Saudi-Arabian Sheikh. He told me in Arabic how the Turkish cavalry desecrated the Holy Shrines of Mecca with their horses' droppings when they rode in to confiscate the sacred relics and transport them to Istanbul.

We returned to the new city via the two-level, sixty-year-old Galata Bridge, which connects the old and new parts of Istanbul. More than 100,000 vehicles cross the upper level of the bridge every day. Restaurants and fruit shops occupy the lower level. On the way to the hotel we visited the covered Oriental Bazaar, where leather goods, jewelry, rugs, antique art and brass gather dust outside the shops. Most of the stuff exhibited is fit for the flea market. A connoisseur may find an object of value, but he will have to pay an unreasonably high price for it.

After lunch we took a cruise on the Bosphorus on a commuter ship near the Galata Bridge. It went as far as the entrance to the Black Sea, where it made a U-turn and stopped at the ancient villages on the European and Asiatic coasts. Each village proudly exhibited its mosque and minaret. I met a German engineer on the ship, who was sent by his company to supervise the building of a steel mill for Turkey. He told me that he spent a few pleaseant years as a German prisoner-of-war in Fort Riley, Kansas. He and his comrades had a free hand in running the military camp and were issued passes and transportation to visit the neighboring American towns without supervision. When they were returned to Germany at the end of World War II, the American general at Fort Riley was sorry to lose such a well disciplined and dedicated group of helpers.

Having been the capital of two empires (the Byzantine and Ottoman Empires), Istanbul (Constantinople) offers many historical sites for scholars and other travelers. It has many palaces (seraglios), museums, beaches, hundreds of churches converted to mosques, and so on. In Uscutar (Scutari), on the Asian coast of Istanbul, is the widely known hospital made famous during the Crimean War by Florence Nightingale, founder of modern nursing. The building is now a military barracks. The lamp that brought her the title "Lady of the Lamp" can still be seen in the same room where it was used.

On our third day in Istanbul we got up early and went to the Mass celebrated by the Armenian Catholic Archbishop. After Mass we met Father Anton (the legal assistant). He took all the details of George's case from us, and promised to meet us at the hotel the next morning. He said, "I know the right lawyer to handle this case. He's a bit greedy, but he gets good results."

After our meeting with Father Anton we went to see the Jewish lawyer who had originally been recommended to us. He told us his partner would not even touch our case, since it involved terrorist activities.

We next called on the American Consulate to seek advice and help. The American Consul met us in his office. He took note of the cause of our visit and asked us to wait in the parlor while he made inquiries about it. Half an hour later the Consul escorted us from the parlor back to his office. Pointing to an open file on his desk, he told me, "According to our records, your nephew was arrested for terrorist activities. I would advise you not to pursue the case. Take the next plane out of the country. I'd hate to have to visit you in prison."

I said, "This is ridiculous! How dare they arrest me for trying to recruit legal assistance to free my nephew, who is kept in jail without trial?"

The Consul replied, "Mr. Orfali, don't forget that you are in Turkey, where your nephew is considered a terrorist. As his uncle, you too could be considered a terrorist."

I said, "I don't buy this reasoning. I came all the way from the United States on a mission and I intend to follow it up until my nephew is free. Can you please recommend a good lawyer?"

The Consul handed me a sheet of paper, saying, "This is a list of lawyers you can consult. It is against our policy to single out just one. I reiterate that you are wasting your time and money, and may end up in trouble yourself."

At hearing this, Archaluz burst into tears. I quieted her as best I could. Then I thanked the Consul and returned to the hotel.

We found good news waiting for us. A message from Father Anton informed us that he had an appointment for us with the best political lawyer, at ten the next morning. He picked us up at nine and drove us to the lawyer's office in his car.

The law firm was staffed by a male secretary-typist, a younger lawyer, and an older female lawyer, mother of the head of the firm. The secretary typed our answers to some vital questions about George's case and took them to his boss's office. He reappeared fifteen minutes later, saying, "Jewet Effendi will see you now. Please follow me." We were led into a spacious room, well furnished in Ottoman style. A conservatively dressed middle-aged gentleman was seated on the dark side of the room behind a large black desk. He stood up, saying, "Welcome to our modest office." Then, pointing to armchairs beside two bright windows, he continued with a smile, "Please make yourselves comfortable." The light on our side of the room gave him the advantage of being able to study our features while we could barely distinguish his face. Once again, we had to repeat all the details of the case as we knew them. The lawyer kept referring to the secretary's notes. He stopped us from time to time and scribbled additions to these notes. We were impressed by his style and felt as though we were being interrogated in a court of law by a kind and friendly magistrate.

Just as we were finishing, the coffee man appeared as if by well-timed magic. He carried a large, immaculate tray with biscuits, and coffee and tea in decorative cups. These cups were topped by covers of shining brass that looked like gold. The coffee man withdrew noiselessly after placing the tray on a serving table. Now the lawyer came over to our side of the desk. He asked each of us our preference and handed us a cup of coffee or tea with some biscuit on the saucer. Bowing with Oriental courtesy as he handed us our drinks, he said, "May it bring you good health." The coffee man appeared again as soon as we finished the refreshments. He collected the empty cups and departed in a flash.

At this time the lawyer addressed us as follows: "Dear friends! I have enough information from you regarding George's unfortunate case. I will send my young associate to bring me the file from the Law Court. I will scrutinize all the details. Please come back tomorrow at the same time, and I will tell you if I am able to take your case."

It was noon, and we invited Father Anton to have lunch with us at the hotel. He accepted, on the condition that we not eat at our hotel where, he said, "the menu is a mixture of European and Mid-Eastern and satisfies neither taste. I would suggest that we go to a restaurant where you can enjoy genuine national food served in a local environment." We followed his advice and our gastronomical tastes were well rewarded. From that day on we had at least one meal a day in a different restaurant with Father Anton.

The next day we were at Jewet Effendi's once again. He received us with a smile and told us he had decided to defend George, who he thought was illegally detained. He then told us his fees. They were very stiff! They were to be paid in advance, in U.S. dollars and in cash. A large chunk of this money, he said, would be absorbed by "vital incidentals." Luckily I had come well prepared. I counted the U.S. currency notes and placed them on the table in front of Jewet Effendi. He put them in his drawer. No receipt was issued. The coffee man appeared at this time and the ritual of the previous day was re-enacted. Jewet Effendi was all business after the coffee. He told us he had located George in the prison for foreigners, a short distance from Istanbul, and had arranged for us to meet him in the afternoon. His young partner would drive us to the prison and back to Istanbul.

At the prison we met George in the prison director's office, which was put at our disposal for the occasion. After the hugging and kissing, we heard from George that he was arrested a few days after his arrival, at the beach where he was swimming with the girl he met in Vienna. They searched his car and found an Armenian flag, which belonged to his sports club. It was hoisted at sports events. George was the president of the club, and the flag had been in his car when he left Rome. The police took him to court. They accused him of acts of subversion and of being an enemy of the Turkish nation. The judge found him innocent and ordered his release. The police gave him back his belongings and set him free.

As he reached his car, they arrested him again. They kept him at the police station without charging him with any offense. For a few days, he was forced to drive the senior officers to expensive restaurants and night clubs at his expense. This explains his unknown whereabouts at that time! They finally charged him with terrorist activities and transferred him to the prison for foreigners to await trial.

George told us he had hired a lawyer who came to see him in prison, and the only thing the lawyer had done so far was to ask for more money. Our young lawyer told him not to worry about the other lawyer. He had George sign a power of attorney authorizing the law firm of Jewet Effendi to represent him.

Prisoners in Turkey have to pay for their own food. They buy it in a concession shop, leased to the highest bidder. The shopkeeper in turn charges as much as he can get out of the prisoners. Prison guards are ready to perform any service for the prisoners who can pay for it. George sent letters and even cables to Rome through this channel. They were received only after we had left that city.

We gave George the food and clothing we had brought with us. We left him with a lighter heart, knowing our stray boy was alive and full of health and that he would be freed in a short while. We stayed three more days in Istanbul and made several visits to Jewet Effendi's law firm. They were busy arranging a new trial for George.

At this time I noticed that we were being shadowed by Turkish undercover agents wherever we went. On the day we left all our luggage was opened and the contents examined piece by piece. Before boarding the plane we were stopped by the National Security Guard. Archaluz was whisked away, while my hand luggage was examined thoroughly. My pockets were emptied and their contents scrutinized in public. The guards kept addressing me in Turkish. I kept shrugging my shoulders and showed them my American passport, saying, "Please speak English."

They brought Archaluz back and told me I could go. They retained a brass dagger used as a letter opener, claiming it was a weapon. The Alitalia agent intervened, saying, "Hundreds of such daggers are sold openly in the covered market. Give it to me. It will be kept in the custody of the airplane pilot until he reaches Rome."

In the plane Archaluz told me she had had to strip off all her clothes in a room where she was examined by a female guard who spoke Italian. They kept asking her about a letter, written in Italian, that they found in her purse. She kept answering, "That is from my daughter. She sent it from Venice." They let her go when they were unable to find anything suspicious on her. I reclaimed my brass dagger when I saw it in the hands of an Italian customs officer in Rome. He handed it to me, saying derisively, "Were you going to kill some Turks with this?"

From Rome I flew to Amman, Jordan to visit my family and tell them what was accomplished so far. An anxious letter from my wife Stephanie awaited me. She had not heard from me since I left home. I called her right away and put her "au courant" of the developments and assured her of my well-being. I then went to Jerusalem to visit my in-laws. They had heard from Stephanie about my cloak-and-dagger mission to Turkey, and addressed me as "Mr. James Bond."

After leaving Jerusalem, I flew home to the States. I was home for only three weeks. I went back to Istanbul with Archaluz to be present at the court proceedings. George's coming trial created a major turmoil in Turkish nationalist circles, which was whipped up by conservative newspapers. They accused Jewet Effendi of treason for defending "a member of an Armenian terrorist organization working to dismember the Turkish state, to create an independent Armenian state within the present Turkish boundaries." On my visit to Jewet Effendi, he showed me letters that he and his assistant had received, threatening them with death and their families with bodily harm. Despite all these things the law firm did not waver in its determination to proceed with the case. On the contrary, it challenged them to do their utmost to have George declared innocent.

At this time, Jewet Effendi asked me whether I had any ideas he could consider. I said, "In my opinion it is very simple. George came to Turkey legally, with a visa issued to him by the Turkish Consulate of Rome. If he was undesirable, he should have been denied entry into Turkey at the frontier. While in this country, all he did was visit a girl friend and go to the beach with her. He was arrested while lying in the sun. The arresting authorities lost their case in a court of law when the judge found George innocent of the charges. Now they are trying to charge him with the same rehashed crimes. Yet from the time he was found innocent to the present time he had been in the custody of the police. This is called double jeopardy in America. "I am confident that the rights of a defendant are likewise protected by the Turkish Desture (Constitution) promulgated by the late Kemal Ataturk, the respected father of the present Turkish state."

Jewet Effendi reacted with a broad smile, remarking, "You are deep, Jacob Effendi!" (An admirable expression of respect.)

While following the proceedings of the trial inside the courtroom, we heard loud protests, shouting, and national songs from organized groups of nationalist Turks, who were demonstrating all around the courthouse. The reader can imagine our discomfort in this awkward situation. The court was crowded with trial lawyers who came to observe the tactics of Jewet Effendi, an acclaimed jurist. He tore apart the prosecution's allegations and made them look like a bunch of incompetents.

After long deliberation, the panel of three judges decided to free George from prison and place him in the custody of Father Anton, who is a citizen of Turkey and a captain in the reserve army. Judgment was deferred for three months until a final decision should be reached. During this period George was not to leave Turkey without the court's permission. It was 8 P.M. by the time the formalities were over and the court's authorization was issued to Father Anton. We had to pay for a special bailiff to transmit the order of release to the chief of the prison where George was returned into custody. We accompanied the bailiff in Father Anton's car. He delivered the release order to the prison in the presence of Father Anton while Archaluz and I waited outside in the rain.

Father Anton came out at midnight without George. He was told that no more releases of prisoners would be processed that day. As we approached his car, a prison van came out of the prison gate and we heard George's voice calling out in Armenian, "Please save me! I don't know where they are taking me!"

We followed the van, speeding when it speeded and slowing down when it slowed down. It stopped at the Police Headquarters of Istanbul. Father Anton parked his car and we followed him to the building. Police officers with drawn guns surrounded us and demanded to know why we had followed the van. Father Anton explained to them diplomatically that our aim was to help George as ordered by the court of law. We were warned that our action was illegal. They were tempted to shoot us as we followed them, they said, on the suspicion that we wanted to kidnap their prisoner. They advised us to call back at nine the next morning and discuss the matter with the "post commandant."

We phoned Jewet Effendi at his home. He had advised us to call him at any hour, even at night, if we were in urgent need of help. He was full of sympathy and thanked us for calling him. He said he would be on his way to the police headquarters as soon as we hung up. He wanted to prevent the transfer of George to a military camp in Ankara (the capital of Turkey) for trial by a military court, where the death penalty is invariably imposed in cases of terrorism. Jewet Effendi assured us strongly, on his honor, that George would be free by nine the next morning. He gave encouragement to Archaluz and hung up.

At ten the next morning, the prodigal son was delivered into the arms of Archaluz at the law office by the junior lawyer. We left mother and son to comfort each other.

We had a conference in Jewet Effendi's office. He was asking for more money. His "expenses" exceeded his estimate by far, and he would have to dish out more "expenses" before George was finally allowed to leave Turkey. I was forced to make a quick trip to Amman, Jordan, to bring the required sum.

I took the bus from Istanbul to the airport and back on my return. The bus terminal is on a hill overlooking the airport. I took an isolated shortcut path to reach it. I was stopped by a plainclothes security guard who appeared from behind some bushes. He wanted to know what I was doing in that area. I told him I was going to catch the bus to Istanbul. He then asked my nationality. When I said I was an American, he wanted to know whether I was Armenian, Greek, or Arab. I replied, "I am just American." I must have convinced him, for he let me go. He followed me at a distance to make sure I took the bus. God, was I lucky! The large amount of undeclared U.S. currency would have been sufficient reason for my arrest.

I paid a courtesy visit to the Armenian Catholic Archbishop. He welcomed me, saying, "Is that really you, Hagop! I can't believe my eyes. You must be really brave, because I know you're not reckless. I admire your courage."

He must have heard about the way the Turkish Security treated me at the airport on departing and after my first trip. "I wonder," he asked, "what more would you have done if George were your son?"

I thanked him for his kind words and replied, "I don't think I'm doing anything extraordinary. In my opinion everybody would do the same in similar circumstances."

The Turkish state doctrine of "homogeneity" is a bunch of baloney. The state is supposed to be secular, guaranteeing freedom of worship. Instead Moslem religious education is taught in the schools. Non-Moslem clerics are not allowed to wear their garb outside their places of worship. The dervish orders banned in 1925 are still in open existence. The Mevlevi or Mawlawi dervishes (dancing dervishes) have a special status and perform their rites openly. Every village has a mosque; it is the social center of the village. People still wear the traditional baggy trousers in the villages. In small towns, women still cover their faces in public. In the larger villages, men congregate in the teahouse. Attached to the teahouse is a family room, where single men are not allowed.

Premier Menderes, of the Bayar presidency in the early 1970s, was too liberal for the Army officers. When the National Unity Committee toppled the government, Menderes and two of his ministers were hanged. Natural gas and crude oil, discovered in the Aegean Sea, rekindled the rivalry between Turkey and Greece. Both claimed ownership. The military dictatorship of Greece overthrew Archbishop Makarios, president of Cyprus, on July 15, 1974. Turkish armed forces, using arms supplied by NATO for defensive purposes, invaded the northern third of Cyprus, ostensibly to protect the Turkish minority. The Turkish army declared a military occupation of northern Cyprus on September 12, 1980. Great Britain, which guaranteed the independence and security of Cyprus in 1960, when it gave the colony independence, did not live up to its pledge. When the United States Congress resolved to stop sending arms to Turkey because it used them against a fellow member of NATO, Turkish hordes were incited to riot and destroy American property. In their rowdy behavior, they dumped American servicemen crossing the Istanbul Galata Bridge into the sea, to the cheering of the crowd. Turkish security forces, which normally swarm in the area, were conspicuously absent.

When I returned from Jerusalem I met with George. He was recovering from the first shocks of freedom. He began talking about his observation of prison life. For instance, he said, "Drugs are sold openly by the guards. Marijuana joints are cheaper than tobacco cigarettes. The mattresses stink from dirt and sweat, and all kinds of bugs swarm under them. Homosexual relations are common, and are practiced openly. Young boys jailed for minor infractions are kept together with hard-core criminals and exposed to all sorts of abuses. Three Palestinian terrorists, who were arrested at Istanbul Airport for trying to hijack an Israeli plane, are given special treatment and all their wishes are fulfilled, to please the Arab nations that supply Turkey with oil."

George wanted to take us to expensive restaurants, night clubs and casinos, and to introduce us to Istanbul's night life. I wasn't interested. When I refused to go, he called me "old-fashioned." He had taken his guitar with him when he left Rome. He played for us and sang Armenian songs, which I did enjoy.

On our last day, as we were leaving Istanbul, George told us he needed new shoes. The ones he had on were dancing shoes. I had a pair of fancy boots with me, which I had brought in case it rained. George tried them on and they fit, so I gave them to him.

We had no trouble at Istanbul Airport this time, but I was relieved when we were in the air. We had a smooth flight. The next day I took an overnight train from Rome to Paris.

I stopped at Sevres, near Paris, where my oldest brother, Joseph, lives with his French wife and their children. He went to France from Jerusalem in the early 1930s to study medicine. The Germans interned him during World War II as the holder of a British (Palestinian) passport. He married a French girl, Elizabeth, after the war.

The Armenian newspapers in France published my nephew George's escapades and they had told Joseph of their eagerness to meet "the Orfali who went to the Lion's Den to help the prey escape." Of course I categorically refused to be interviewed, in order not to infuriate the Turks at this stage of the affair. I knew that the Turkish Secret Service receives copies of all Armenian newspapers published in the whole world. I flew back home the next day.

From Paris, I flew back to the United States. Was I happy to be back home! All the joints of my body were aching and I felt the beginning of a cold, a consequence of standing in the draft and drizzle while waiting outside the prison gate for George's release. I surrendered to my wife Stephanie's ministrations. She spoiled me, nursed me with loving care, and kept me in the house until I was fully recovered.

George had to stay in Turkey after we left. There was a final session of the court, at which he was sentenced to one year's probation. He was set free on his own recognizance, and was allowed to leave the country. But he was ordered to report back to the court after one year, to hear its final decision. The additional "expenses" paid to the lawyer had done the trick. George finally left Turkey. Naturally, he never went back.

Suleynaniye Mosque in Istanbul.

Typical Turkish village on the Asiatic side of the Bosphorous Straits.

Jacob, Archaluz and Father Anton by the dock of
the Ferry in Istambul.

The Armenian Catholicos (Pope) with the visiting Russian Orthodox Patriarch at the Echmiadzin Cathedral, seat of the Armenian Gregorian Church.

A Visit to Ancestral Armenia

I think we all aspire to visit the lands of our ancestors. Stephanie and I had discussed several times the possibility of visiting modern Armenia, to see Mount Ararat, Erevan (capital of Armenia), and other historic sites. We finally decided last year to join a group tour to the Soviet Union with the A.A.R.P. (American Association of Retired People), to which we belong. (Stephanie served as president for two terms in the Chapter of Zion, Illinois, where we lived before moving to California.)

Our trip was to last twenty-one days, from April 6 to April 27, 1986. The tour included a stay in Erevan and a visit to Mount Ararat and Lake Sevan, as well as Moscow, Tbilisi, Kiev, and Leningrad. We paid a deposit six months in advance, then sent them the balance of the fare, before we received a call from the A.A.R.P. telling us our tour had been canceled because not enough people were interested in traveling to the U.S.S.R. so early in the year.

Luckily, we knew the same tour was being offered by General Tours of New York. They were happy to accommodate us. We arrived in Moscow on April 7, 1986.

We were welcomed by Natasha, a smartly dressed, attractive young Russian woman. She introduced herself, saying, "I will be your travel manager during your stay in the U.S.S.R." When we had finished with the formalities of customs, she checked our names with her list and took us to the Cosmos Hotel in a special bus assigned to us by the Intourist. On the way she told us we had been assigned bus number 60, which carried a special guide who would show us all the points of interest in Moscow. Thereafter we would have a different bus in every city we visited, each with a local guide to show us around. When we were given rooms in the hotel, each person was handed a hotel tag with his or her name and room number. We were to carry these tags with us for identification, as well as to help us find our way to the hotel if we got lost in the city. This same procedure was followed in all the cities we visited.

An hour later, after washing and changing our clothes, we met in the hotel dining room. Here we were offered a very substantial dinner. The appetizer was a cold plate of fish, cheese, pickles, and several kinds of bread. This was followed by soup, steak, potatoes and a vegetable, beer and soft drinks, coffee or tea, and cake for dessert. This was typical of the fare we were served for lunch and dinner during our stay. For breakfast we usually had boiled or fried eggs, olives, cheese, and jam with coffee or tea. The hotels were first-rate and the service was good.

Our first visit in Moscow was to the Kremlin, or "citadel," the capital of Russia. We were amazed at the ease of access to the Kremlin compound. Nobody checked our identities or searched us, and we were able to circulate freely and even to take pictures whenever we liked.

We saw the three principal cathedrals of Uspensky (Assumption), Blagoveshchensky (Annunciation), and Arkangelsky (Archangel Michael), and the Bell Tower of Ivan the Great. We were able to visit the inside of only one cathedral, so we chose the Annunciation Cathedral. We were awed by the way everything — the icons, the altars, the paintings — was restored with skill and patience, and apparently with no concern for the cost in time or money. Our guide explained to us that as national historic sites, these cathedrals are protected by the Soviet constitution and preserved as an inheritance for future generations.

We saw the world's largest bell. It had never rung, because it fell and broke while being installed. We also saw the largest cannon of its time, which had never been fired.

We visited the Congress Hall, the only modern building in the Kremlin, and watched a ballet performance in its auditorium. We went to Red Square, saw St. Basil's Cathedral, watched the changing of the guard, visited Lenin's mausoleum, saw the Gum (the largest department store) and the Bolshoi Theatre. We traveled to the circus on the Metro (the Moscow subway), and took pictures of the decor in the stations. Each station is an individual work of art. Some stations looked like palaces, with marble columns and intricate mosaics.

On our last night in Moscow we were taken to a plush farewell party in the largest hotel. We were served black and red caviar, cold cuts, salads, wine, champagne, vodka, beer, soft drinks, shashlik, and fruits while we enjoyed the music of a full band. This celebration was repeated at every town we visited.

Our next stop was Erevan, the capital of Armenia. We arrived at the Moscow airport shortly after eleven in the morning, and were told our plane would be leaving at seven that night. We wondered what had caused this confusion. Later we learned that there are two daily flights from Moscow to Erevan, one at 11 A.M. and one at 7 P.M., and that somehow the Moscow Intourist office had booked us on the wrong one. But this gave us a chance to explore the huge domestic airport of Moscow. It was congested with passengers from all over the U.S.S.R. We observed that the waiting rooms for the local people were a far cry from those used by visiting foreigners like ourselves. Ours had ample space, armchairs, sofas, and plenty of propaganda to read.

In our lounge, we saw a group of Syrians who were carrying singing birds in cages. Their Intourist guide was a young Armenian woman. She told me they were completing their visit to the U.S.S.R. by taking an Aeroflot plane home from Erevan, which has direct flights to Syria.

When we boarded our 7 P.M. flight, it was overcrowded with Armenians returning to Erevan, each carrying large bundles of goods purchased in Moscow. My Armenian seatmate struck up a conversation with me, and was surprised when I answered him in Armenian. I told him that I was from the United States and that this was my first visit to Armenia. One of the young men said, "It's a shame you've waited so long to visit the land of your ancestors." Another young man, wearing a military uniform and medals dangling on his chest, offered me a chocolate bar. I cut off two small pieces, one for Stephanie and one for me, and gave back the rest to him with a pack of chewing gum. They were all friendly, smartly dressed and well informed about life in the United States. Many had relatives in Los Angeles.

We reached Hotel Armenia in Erevan well after 11 P.M. The restaurant was closed, and we were told that no food would be served until breakfast in the morning. I took charge and demanded to see the manager. When he arrived, I said, "Here I am, a stranger in the land of my ancestors. I spoke so highly of this place to my fellow travelers from America, and now this hotel denies us the traditional Armenian hospitality by withholding food from us when we are hungry."

"I am sorry, brother," he said, "but the restaurant is closed."

"Is the bar closed?" I asked. "How about some beer, cold cuts, and soft drinks?"

The manager could not find strong enough words to express his regret for not having thought of a way to make us comfortable. He disappeared for a short time, then returned with a train of waiters who carried dishes full of different cold cuts — sausages, pastrami, cheese, pickles, and glasses for beer and Pepsi-Cola, which were also brought in great quantities. Despite our prodigious hunger, there were plenty of leftovers

when we had eaten our fill. By the time we retired to our rooms
it was past one in the morning.

There are many legends about Erevan. One of them tells us
that the word "ereval" means "it appears" in Armenian, and
that this was what Noah exclaimed when he first saw land,
before the waters of the Great Flood receded and his ark perched
on Mount Ararat. Another legend says that Erevan was the
home of the Eri tribe. It is now the capital of the Soviet
Armenian Republic, with a population of over a million, and is
the major industrial and cultural center of Armenia. Erevan is
one of the real ancient towns. It is older than Rome or Athens.
It is contemporary with Nineveh and Babylon. Its ancient origin
is attested by a cuneiform inscription on a basalt slab, which says
that in 782 B.C., "Argistis, son of Manua, founded this town of
Erebuni to the glory of the land of Bianili and to instill fear in
his enemies." Erebuni was an important center of the Urartu
kingdom in the Eighth Century B.C. Its inhabitants traded with
Greece, Rome and Egypt.

We met our Armenian guide the next day at breakfast. He
was a sympathetic young man who spoke perfect English and
was very knowledgeable. After we got to know him, he told us
that he had visited Havana and East Germany. He took us on a
tour of the city. Native tuffa stone of many different shades of
pink is used to build houses in Erevan. They are quite beautiful.
The climate of Erevan is semi-tropical. Its parks have many
sparkling fountains, which bring relief to the city during the hot
dry summers. The industrial district is downwind from the city
to spare it from air pollution.

We drove to Etchmiazin, the seat of the Catholicos, who is
the head of the Armenian Gregorian church. Etchmiazin is
fifteen kilometers from Erevan. Vardkesavan was a settlement
established here in the Third Century B.C. Its name was later
changed to Vagarshapat.

History tells us the Roman Emperor Diocletian chose
Rhipsime, a fair Christian girl, for his bride. Because he was a
pagan she refused him, and fled to Armenia with some other
Christians. They came to Vagarshapat, where they preached
their religion. The Roman Emperor asked Tridates III, the Tsar
or ruler of Armenia, to send Rhipsime back. However, when
Tridates saw her, he proposed to her himself. She refused him,
because he too was a pagan. In his anger, Tridates had Rhipsime
and her friends stoned to death. After this event he lost his
mind, believing himself to be a wild boar. Saint Gregory, who
was imprisoned for being a Christian, cured Tridates' madness

and converted him and the whole Armenian nation to Christianity in the year 301 A.D. Chapels were built in memory of Rhipsime and Gayane, another martyred girl. Other churches were built over pagan temples dedicated to gods of fire, water and so on. Gregory had a vision of Christ descending to the earth. He struck the earth with a golden hammer, and an image of a church appeared. Gregory erected Etchmiazin Cathedral on the site in 303 A.D. The name means "The Descent of the Only Begotten." Thus the name of Vagarshapat was changed again, this time to Etchmiazin. Gregory was later canonized. He is known as St. Gregory the Illuminator. At Zvarnots, just two kilometers from Erevan, we saw the ruins of St. Gregory's cathedral. Built in the Seventh Century, it collapsed in the Tenth.

Mesrob Mashtot created the Armenian alphabet in the Fourth Century A.D. and translated the Bible into Armenian. The Armenian Gregorian Church is monophysite. This doctrine holds that Christ was pure spirit, without a physical body. At present, religion is not encouraged, but people are free to worship in their churches. We witnessed a baptism in progress in one of the churches.

The northern districts of Erevan are largely settled by Armenian repatriates, survivors of the Holocaust, and their offspring who have returned from the Diaspora. These settlements are called Nor-Arabkir (New Arabkir), Nor-Zeitun (New Zeitun), and so on; these are names of towns in Western Armenia where some Armenians survived the Turkish genocide.

I took a trip on my own to Matenadaran Library. It contains 13,000 items, some of them very old. There are works of historians, astronomers, mathematicians, philosophers; manuscripts in Armenian, Persian, Latin, Greek, Arabic and Hebrew.

One night we had a wine-tasting session in the wine cellar of the hotel. Our California Napa wines are much better, but we enjoyed the anecdotes with which the winemaster accompanied each wine we tasted.

The next day we were told that instead of traveling to Tbilisi (Georgia) by bus as planned, we would fly there directly because the roads were blocked by snow. This was unfortunate. The bus would have given us the chance to see the beautiful Lake Sevan, located 1,900 meters above sea level, one of the largest mountain lakes in the world. We would also have had a closer look at Mount Ararat, which is sacred to all Armenians, and is now in Turkish territory.

At nine in the morning we were taken by bus to Garni, twenty-eight kilometers from Erevan. On the way we stopped at a monument to Egishe Tcharents, a well-known Armenian poet. We had a good view of the snow-covered Mount Massis (the Armenian name for Mount Ararat). It reminded me of Noah's legendary exclamation, "Ereval!" when he first sighted land, before his boat came to rest on Mount Ararat. I was now doing the opposite by gazing upon Ararat from a point close to Erevan.

Garni, built in the Third Century B.C., was a famous Armenian fortress. It is mentioned by Tacitus. Destroyed by Rome in 59 A.D., it was rebuilt by Tridates I, who defeated the Romans, went to Rome, and received a compensation of 150 million dinars and a crown from Nero. In 1679 A.D. an earthquake finished off what remained of Garni after its destruction at the hands of the Turks in 1638.

At Garni a temple was re-created of stones from the excavations begun in 1949. The Armenian kings used to come here in the summer and reside in what they called the Cool Palace. Nearby are remains of the Royal Baths. They had mosaic floors and hot air circulated in ceramic pipes beneath the floors.

We proceeded to Gueghard, thirty-eight kilometers from Erevan. It was formerly called Airivank ("Monastery of Caves"), and dates from pre-Christian times. The church was built between the Tenth and Thirteenth Centuries. It was called Gueghard ("lance" in Armenian) because it was believed that the lance that pierced the body of Christ was kept in this church. The lance is now kept in the museum of Etchmiazin Cathedral. Besides the monastery building, there are three churches cut into the rock in Gueghard. The Avazan church in particular is a unique work of art. A deeper church in the rock shows a coat of arms consisting of the head of an ox, two bound lions and, between the lions, an eagle clutching a lamb in its claws. All these are hewn into the rock. Inside the church are a fountain and a pool of miraculous water. I saw an Armenian mother drink from the fountain and wash her face and limbs, and those of her child, in the water from the pool.

In the park of the monastery is a special place where the blessed sheep are sacrificed, skinned and cut for the familes that bring them. Sometimes a sheep is owned by more than one family, and when it is sacrificed it is divided equally among them. Some families sacrifice roosters. One of our fellow travelers asked one of the owners whether they eat the sacrifice or give it to the poor. The owner replied, "We eat it. We are all poor."

Gueghard is a shrine for pilgrims. Those who come here tie a bit of cloth to one of the trees before leaving, in memory of having been in this sacred place.

In the afternoon, after returning to our hotel for lunch, we visited the Armenian National History Museum in Lenin Square. It was filled with artifacts, paintings, sculptures and so on, depicting the history of Armenian civilization through the ages. A very moving Memorial to the Victims of the 1915 Massacre, located on top of Tsizernakaberd Park, was created with twelve pylons in a circle, leaning against each other. As one looks at them, one has the impresion of seeing people with their arms around one another's shoulders, their heads bent in silence. An eternal flame burns within the monument, accompanied by impressive funeral music by the Armenian composers Komidas and Yekmalian.

On our last night in Erevan we watched a musical performance of Armenian folk music, with instruments, a full mixed choir, a large group of male and female dancers, and skits. The performance lasted over two hours with a fifteen-minute intermission. The music was enjoyable, the various regional costumes dazzling, and the performers excellent.

Everywhere we traveled, people went out of their way to be helpful to us. One of our companions was looking with interest at the entrance to a theatre. An usher spotted him and insisted on admitting him free. A taxi driver refused to accept the fare from another of our friends.

We soon acquired a general familiarity with present-day Armenia and its people. I quote from the tourist pamphlet *Armenia*: "Soviet Armenia occupies 0.13 percent of the landmass of the Soviet Union and has 1.1 percent of its population. And yet it accounts for between 5 and 35 percent of the national production of many types of industrial goods, including molybdenum, copper sulfate, carbide, acetic acid, synthetic rubber, mobile electric power stations, power transformers, centrifugal pumps and metal-cutting lathes. The most developed industries are electrical engineering, instrument-making and electronics."

The Soviet Union's MIG planes are named after Migoyan, an Armenian aeronautic engineer, brother of Anastas Mikoyan, former prominent leader and member of the Politburo of the U.S.S.R. Armenian stonemasons were famous throughout history. St. Germain-des-Pres and the belfry of Charlemagne's palace in Aachen were built by Oton Matsaetsi in 806–811. Armenian masons repaired the dome of Ste. Sophia in Constantinople and built the Church of San Satiro in Milan. The illustrations in three medallions of the Noah's ark story, and Zvarnots Cathedral in the Royal St. Chapelle church of Paris are the work of Armenians.

I would have liked to see more of Armenian life in the villages and cooperative farms, but our time was limited. The guide suggested that I visit Armenia again with an Armenian group, to spend more time and see everything I wish.

We flew to Tbilisi from Erevan in a tiny plane, experiencing several bumps caused by air pockets. One of the passengers was a Jewish female professor who taught in Brooklyn, New York. She was visiting the U.S.S.R. as a representative of the American educational system. We met her again later in Tbilisi, in the company of educators from the Soviet Republic of Georgia.

The Georgian people were very friendly and helpful. Several incidents impressed me. The handle of my suitcase was broken in Moscow Airport. I was unable to have it repaired in Moscow, Erevan, or Tbilisi. I mentioned this to a fellow traveler who had visited the Soviet Union several times before. "I will mention it to a friend in Tbilisi," he said. "He will certainly find someone to repair it." When we returned to the hotel after visiting the town of Tbilisi, I got a message asking me to stop at the service office. When I got there, I was handed a brand-new suitcase with wheels, made in Czechoslovakia. On another occasion, I was buying some stationery in the old city of Tbilisi. A customer standing next to me told the saleswoman, "I am paying for his purchase." I was astounded, and protested that I could not accept his offer. He responded in German: "Comrade, when I was in Germany they treated me very well." He must have mistaken me for a German!

After Tbilisi, we flew to Sochi, the "Russian Riviera" on the Black Sea, then to Kiev in the Ukraine, where I was given medicine for my sore throat and ointment for the arthritis in my right shoulder. Both medicines were effective, and both were dirt cheap.

We ended up in Leningrad, having visited all the places of interest in the towns on the way. Our hotel accommodations, food and service were first-rate. What impressed me most was the feeling of total security everywhere and at all times. We met people, old and young, men and women, walking all alone in deserted streets at one or two in the morning. They carried bags; they were unafraid of being molested. Traffic laws were strictly enforced. Two of our bus drivers were ticketed for speeding, one on the Georgian highways and the other in Leningrad. The cleanliness, even in the big cities, was amazing. Graffiti was unheard of.

The people were friendly and cordial everywhere. And everywhere, they told us that they want peace with the United States, and want to be left alone to live their lives in their own way.

Old Armenian lady, survivor of the Turkish genocide.

Monument to the Armenian victims of the genocide, with modern Erevan in
the background.

High-tech chemical plant in Soviet Armenia.

Traditional Armenian dances performed in Erevan.

Originally built in Third Century B.C., the ancient Armenian temple of Garni was reconstructed from the ruins.

Israeli soldiers and orthodox Jews in prayer shawls mingle with children, shoppers and Arabs wearing *kafies* outside the Damascus Gate of the Old City of Jerusalem.

Jerusalem Today

Young Israelis are as determined as ever to accomplish their dream of making Israel a model democratic country. In many ways, Israel is a haven for world Jewry where they can enjoy the latest conveniences, and most advanced medical facilities. However, there is another side of the coin.

On my recent visit to Jerusalem, my city of birth, I was fortunate to meet a number of persons I knew during the British Mandate over Palestine. The following is a sampling of the views expressed by the people living under the present Israeli rule.

Shimson, a Jew, came to the Christian Brothers' College from the Alliance Israelite School which was sponsored by the French government. We got along well. Shimson was a liberal. He spoke to me about the differences in the Jewish community. He hated the ultra-conservative Hassidic Jews and called them "disruptive parasites and cowards who never worked in their life, but lived on money sent to Jerusalem by the world Jewry." These are the trouble makers, who feel they are ordained to implement the laws of the Sabbath. They stone the cars that dare to pass near their quarters from Saturday eve to Sunday eve. There are rumors that the Hassids continued to practice polygamy secretly, they consider their additional women as maids. A Hassidic sect still venerates Shabbetai Zevi who was born in Smyrna, Turkey, in 1626, and was ordained a rabbi at the age of eighteen. Shabbetai proclaimed himself the Messiah, and had Jewish followers all over the world, even after he converted to Islam in 1666. His prophet, Nathan of Gaza told the Messiah's followers that the conversion to Islam is a profound mystery. It would be made clear in time. Shabbetai died on the Day of Atonement, September 17, 1676. The believers in Shabbetai are called underground Jews. They meet secretly to speak of their Messiah and to engage in licenscious heterosexual and homosexual behavior.

After graduation from college, Shimson got an administrative job with the British Mandate in Jerusalem. He was appointed head of his department by the State of Israel in 1948 and was retired when I met him this time. He was the same old firebrand Shimson, he did not hesitate to express his dissatisfaction with the present situation in Israel. He said,

"Could you imagine that my grandson has joined the disruptive zealots?" He then went on, "Do you know what the zealots want? They aim that Israel should go back to the primitive life as practiced prior to the destruction of the second temple in 70 A.D. They already forced the Israel government to impose the kosher laws in public places. A train passenger is denied milk in his coffee or tea with a salami sandwich, to avoid mixing milk with meat as prescribed by the kosher laws (The Kashrut)." These laws are the distorted interpretations of some over eager self-proclaimed experts of the mosaic commands which among other things says, "Do not cook the lamb in its mother's milk." Shimson proceeded to tell me things a Jew would not tell to a non-Jew. Such as, how the newly arrived Russian Jews are very difficult to satisfy, in spite of the fact that they are given preferential treatment. Many of them would like to go back to the U.S.S.R. where the government did the thinking for them. They cannot adjust to the idea of the competition in a free society. He also told me about the over-abundance of college graduates in Israel. Graduates are forced to leave the country and accept jobs in Canada, Australia or the U.S.A. He mentioned that many of the American immigrants to Israel (Olim or Ascenders in Hebrew) are going back (Yordim or Descenders in Hebrew). Finally Shimson said, "We would survive these hard times, if our oddball spoilers, the Hassidim, the believers in Shabbetai Zevi, and the Zealots, would let us. Do you know, Jacob, that these crazies have the nerve to knock at the doors of people who watch television and order them to get rid of the set, as to watch pictures on the screen in the Holy City of Jerusalem is against the Jewish law? Does this not remind you of the Fanatics versus the Moderates in the *War with Rome: Jerusalem* by Josephus Flavius? I am really scared of the future. Could you imagine religious fanatics burning a bus station where advertising posters showed scantily dressed women, and the retaliations of burning a synagogue and defacing the building with swastikas, by Jews here in the state of Israel?"

In the old city I met Ismael, a Moslem fellow student from the same Christian Brothers' College. He later went to Al Azhar Moslem religious school in Cairo. He is now in the administration of the WAKF, Moslem Estates. He complained about the tight restrictions imposed on the non-Jews by the Israelis. What hurt him most were the derogatory remarks of "ALLAH," the name of God in Arabic, made by Jewish military personnel. He wondered whether they knew that it is the same name as "ILUHIM," the Hebrew name of God, to whom Moses was introduced by his father-in-law Jethro the Arab Sheikh. He also complained that the State of Israel confiscated all the land owned by Arabs around Jerusalem and built apartments for Jewish immigrants. He told me that due to the fall in oil prices, the Palestinian Arabs were fired by the oil rich Arab states and were replaced by cheap Pakistani and South Korean labor.

The Palestinian Arabs sent their earning to their folks in the West Bank. Now that this has stopped, it is aggravating the already unenviable situation of these people. What worried Ismael most was the fate of the workers who were fired. They have no prospect of other jobs. In their despair some of them join the ranks of the freedom fighters.

At the Armenian Quarter I met some old friends, survivors of the genocide who came to Jerusalem as refugees after World War I. They became successful business men. They bought property and built homes in the suburbs of Jerusalem. Their children became doctors, engineers, government and bank employees. Most of the young generation of Armenians were forced to leave Jerusalem after the Israel occupation. They could not put up with being treated as second class citizens, and they had no job opportunities. Many are now in the U.S.A., Canada, Australia and Europe. The older generation is back at the Armenian convent, where they started when they came as refugees. The homes they had built in the suburbs were confiscated by the State of Israel as enemy property, though the Armenians never declared war or fought against Israel. They are considered as former enemy subjects because they traveled on passports issued by the Jordanian occupation authorities. Those Armenians who stayed in Jerusalem are all hardworking business men. They don't discourage easily, but grind their teeth and hope to overcome the adversity. A well-respected old Armenian whom I visited in Jerusalem told me, "Jacob, the followers of the old Jewish prophets, of Jesus and of Mohammed have all conquered this land. Could it be that the followers of Lenin, the workers' prophet, will be next in line?" There have been Armenians in Jerusalem for over 1,500 years and they will be in the Holy City for at least another 1,500 years if it is still there.

I am very happy to be back home in our peaceful Napa city, away from the turmoil and unending international intrigues of the Middle East.

About the Author

Jacob George Orfali (Hagop Khatcherian) was born of Armenian parents in Jerusalem in 1915 during the Ottoman rule. He grew up amid the cultural diversity under the British Mandate of Palestine, and was educated at the Christian Brothers' College in the Holy City. Jacob worked as a translator at the Jerusalem Police Headquarters under the British Administration. Later he was a traveling auditor for the Socony Vacuum Oil Company in Jerusalem, Beirut and Damascus. Jacob reorganized the accounting classification system for the United Nations Headquarters at UNESCO in Beirut. In São Paulo, Brazil he was cost engineer for hydroelectric power station projects with the São Paulo Light and Power and member of the Brazilian Standards Association. At Abbott Laboratories in north Chicago, Jacob served as cost accountant. Later he worked for the U.S. Postal Service in Zion, Illinois. Fluent in nine languages, which he acquired while interacting with people from many cultures, Jacob Orfali's philosophy is that people of diverse background and experience have the same aspirations and essential human nature. "Everywhere you go, people are the same!" He and his wife Stephanie now make their home in Napa, California.